To Lois,

May Love Always

Marie

The Power of the Dream

The Power of the Dream

Looking Forward in the Later Years

Marie White Webb

Marie White Webb

DIMENSIONS
FOR LIVING
NASHVILLE

The Power of the Dream
Looking Forward in the Later Years

This book is printed on recycled, acid-free, elemental-chlorine–free paper.

ISBN 0-687-07532-7

99 00 01 02 03 04 05 06 07 08—10 9 8 7 6 5 4 3 2 1

MANUFACTURED IN THE UNITED STATES OF AMERICA

To

Richard H. Gentzler, Jr.
who is inspiring so many with
the Dream in older adult years,

and

To

My Children and Grandchildren
who help keep me looking forward.

Contents

Dreams of Peace

Foreword

Young people often speak of living on the edge. I think they are trying to describe what it is like to walk up to the threshold of every new experience with courage and curiosity and then to make the most of it and to take it all in stride. Marie Webb is a perfect example of this kind of courageous living. She does a marvelous job of telling the story of life in simple, beautiful and touching images. She has distilled the wisdom of three quarters of a century of faithful living and made it readily accessible to all who walk with her in the journey of growing older. These pages reflect the maturity, peace and wisdom of one who walks in conscious companionship with the Author of life. It is a companionship that brings courage, hope and joy to the journey we all make.

As you read these pages you will discover that the story Marie Webb is telling is your story. Whether you define yourself as young or old you are growing older, and you will find yourself here. Your hopes, your fears, your sorrows, your joys and your dreams will resonate with the reflections on life found in these pages. These stories are about one women's incredible spiritual journey but you will discover that underneath is the universal story of the journey of life from birth to death that we all travel.

The mystery of life cannot be measured or contained in carefully constructed arguments. But now and then we get a glimpse into the mystery and we see the goodness, richness, excitement, joy and hope that makes up the journey of life for us all. These pages help us to see some of the goodness hidden in the autumn days of the mystery of life. These pages are filled with realism. The stories here do not avoid the painful experiences of life. They are faced and reported honestly and reverently. The shadow side of life is not overlooked or ignored. Every facet of life is accepted and considered as a gift from the hand of God. In this way, even the painful experiences are woven into the beautiful and strong fabric of life lived fully under the watchful and loving gaze of God.

Every age and stage in life has its peculiar limitations. Growing older has its share of limitations and to deny them is to miss a part of the richness of living well. The limitations of any age are best met with courage, hope and above all else a sense of humor. Marie Webb lets us see the courage, hope and humor at work in her life as she shares a portion of her journey of life with us. Each story reminds us that life is good because God is good and all things are possible with God.

Bishop Rueben P. Job

Preface

Power of the Dream in the Autumn of Life

The theme song of the 1996 Olympics began with the words: "It is the power of the dream that brings us here." Surely, not many young athletes would have started on the road to Atlanta if had it not been for their dreams.

But there are us old athletes, too, on the highway of life. We had dreams of many kinds. Too many of us have given up to sit by the wayside, waiting for our earthly lives to end. God can help us to reconnect with those dreams.

My husband, Lance, and I moved into a private apartment in a retirement center where we spent the last two winters before he died in 1995 at age eighty-six. He was determined to keep alive, to keep moving, even after suffering a broken hip. I was helping him with his walker to enter the dining room when another resident stopped us. The woman was quite stooped, and her eyes were listless as she twisted her face upward and announced: "It takes guts to get old!" Her face haunts me. How I wish that I had tried in some way to bring hope and courage back to her mind.

Just how can we discover the power of the dream? Through observation and experience, but most of all from the admonitions and promises of the Scriptures we can discover the power of the dream. When Peter preached his great sermon on the Day of Pentecost, he quoted from Joel 2:28: "Your old men (*women, too!*) shall dream dreams."

As I contemplate the last quarter of my life—the autumn time for me—I am challenged by the words of the psalmist in "A Harvest of Joy":

> ... We were like those who dream.
> Then our mouth was filled with laughter
> and our tongue with shouts of joy;
> then it was said among the nations,
>   "The Lord has done great things for them."
>
> (Psalm 126:1-2)

Yes, the Lord has done great things for me, even through two devastating losses. Jim, my husband of fifty years, died in 1990. I lost Lance, my second husband, just five years later. But that is why the Psalmist's prayer is mine:

> May those who sow in tears
>   reap with shouts of joy.
> Those who go out weeping,
>   bearing the seed for sowing,
> shall come home with shouts of joy,
>   carrying their sheaves. (Psalm 126:5-6)

And so it is that we sow in the sunshine and also in the shadows, "Fearing neither clouds nor winter's chilling breeze, ... We shall go rejoicing, bringing in the sheaves."

Dreams of Hope

1 *Musings on the Deck*

It is early autumn in the Ozarks. The leaves of oak and maple and ash are beginning to drift down upon my deck. The wooded bluffs above and beyond Beaver Lake, as the sun strikes them, begin to glow with rich colors of orange, red, and yellow, highlighted by the lingering green. One little sailboat drifts aimlessly on the lake.

Yesterday, the outlook was different. Drizzling rain fell all day long. I felt the full force of my seventy-six years, alone in the house where I watched Lance die just one year ago. An unusual sadness darkened my spirits, and I felt lonely.

Today is a new day. The sun rose in all its brilliance dispelling the fog and clouds. I remember that one-fourth of my life may remain if I am lucky enough to escape accident, heart disease, and cancer.

Because my heavenly Father watches over me, I am not drifting like that sailboat or—to change metaphors—crouching by the side of the road. God remains my guide and my companion. I still have some dreams, and I want others to realize their dreams, too.

Two hummingbirds are still greedily sipping nectar at my feeders. Just a short time ago there were two dozen. I watched them compete for a place to drink before they flew away. Why did two stay longer? Until they, too, gain enough strength to fly 500 miles south? They will surely follow nature's timetable.

I am tempted to wonder sometimes why I am still here, when dear friends and relatives have gone ahead of me. Does our Creator have a plan for me?

Help me, O God, to be able to carry in some harvest sheaves during the autumn of life.

Sowing in the morning, sowing seeds of kindness,
Sowing in the noontide and the dewy eve;
Waiting for the harvest, and the labor ended,
We shall come rejoicing, bringing in the sheaves.

Autumn can be a beautiful and rewarding season or it can be a gloomy time. It all depends on our attitude and commitment. Sometimes we may feel that we are working under sunset skies, that we should be able now to sit and do nothing. But the promise and command come: "For God is not unjust; he will not overlook your work and the love that you showed for his sake in serving the saints, as you still do. And we want each one of you to show the same diligence so as to realize the full assurance of hope to the very end" (Hebrews 6:10-11).

2 Gathering the Autumn Fruit

Having grown up on an Illinois farm before the Rural Electrification Association brought magical electrical lines to the countryside, I can remember the preparations in autumn so that family and livestock would have food and warmth for the winter. Several bushels of apples, potatoes, onions, and other root crops, were stored in the fruit cellar. Apple butter, which simmered all day long outside in the big copper-lined black kettle, joined the rows of jellies and jars of peaches, cherries, and blackberries canned earlier in the year, not to mention the green beans and stewed tomatoes.

Out in the fields, Dad let the two-horse team pull the lumber wagon through the rows of corn as he and the hired hand shucked the ears of corn. They shelled enough corn for storage in the barn alongside the granary-rooms of oats and wheat, knowing that timothy hay was overhead in the loft. They hauled wood for heating and cooking from the timber, sawed and split it, and stacked it on the woodpile. We all raked leaves as we washed and put up the storm windows.

It would not be many years until tractors and combines, home freezers, and furnaces would change our way of life, but still there were preparations for winter. A quiet, peaceful time came after the hard work of summer.

There are changes, too, when we reach the autumn of life, not only in the world about us, but also in our bodies. As the days grow shorter, we are aware that our time on earth is getting shorter.

In Plato's *Republic*, we read that Socrates inquired of his friend Cephalus about the journey of life. He asked whether the road is smooth and easy or rugged and difficult. Is life harder toward the end? The old man assured Socrates that "old age has a great sense of calm and freedom."

Elton Trueblood, writing on "The Blessings of Maturity," quoted the above conversation and then added his own observations: "Never ignoring or denying the physical hardships of old age, I nevertheless affirm that . . . the calmness and freedom of which Cephalus spoke are real! The fact that autumn is, in many ways, the most beautiful season of the year is a parable of life, as well as a fact of nature."[1]

Trueblood summarized his thoughts, "Each added day affords me an opportunity to remember some event or person, already partly forgotten, but now recovered with vividness. This is what we mean by gathering of the autumn fruits without the sense of urgency which was inevitable when the plants, destined to produce fruits, were being watered, nurtured, and tended."[2]

Life may seem more calm, but it still takes a lot of effort to harvest certain fruits. They are "love, joy, peace, patience, kindness, generosity, faithfulness, gentleness and self-control" (Ephesians 5:22). I have a lot of work to do in my older years!

3 Miles to Go Before I Sleep

I now live in the Missouri-Arkansas Ozarks, not too far from the place where Harold Bell Wright wrote *The Shepherd of the Hills.* He began his story thus: "In the hills of life there are two trails. One lies along the higher sunlit fields where those who journey see afar, and the light lingers even when the sun is down; and one leads to the lower ground, where those who travel, as they go, look always over their shoulders with eyes of dread, and gloomy shadows gather long before the day is done."[1]

One of the Sunday school songs that we used to sing in our little country church ended with these words:

> I want to scale the utmost height,
> And catch a gleam of glory bright;
> But still I'll pray till Heav'n I've found,
> Lord, lead me on to higher ground.

Surely life should be an ascension from birth to life triumphant. There are valleys and hard places, of course. Some stop in the valleys; when they give up, they don't try as hard. Lacking a vision and determination, they might agree with Dante, who wrote:

In the middle of the journey of our life
I came to myself within a dark wood
Where the straight way was lost.[2]

It's possible to get lost, to go in circles, in the woods. But instead of describing the last part of life as a "dark wood," I prefer the picture painted by Robert Frost:

The woods are lovely, dark and deep.
But I have promises to keep,
And miles to go before I sleep.[3]

Sometimes we do get weary along the way as grief and disappointments come, but we have this reassurance:

The LORD is the everlasting God,
  the Creator of the ends of the earth.
He does not faint or grow weary;
  his understanding is unsearchable.
He gives power to the faint, and strengthens the powerless.
Even youths will faint and be weary,
  and the young will fall exhausted;
but those who wait for the LORD shall renew their strength,
  they shall mount up with wings like eagles,
they shall run and not be weary,
  they shall walk and not faint.

(Isaiah 40:28-31)

4 Age Challenged

What does it mean to be old? To have less value than previously? To be considered all alike, a burden to society?

I have participated in an image game in workshop groups. I have also tried it with adult Sunday school classes. Ask them for words that first come to their minds that describe *oldness*. A few are positive—grandparents, experience, wisdom, endurance, happy, and fun. But most words are negative—wrinkles, gray hair, slow, cane, glasses, hearing aid, dentures, new parts, pain, confusion, forgetfulness, loneliness, senile, blind, tinkle, deaf, and stooped.

Usually only about 12 percent of images are positive. Physicians are the worst, and nurses are not much better. They thought that 70 percent of people over sixty-five are in nursing homes, whereas only 5 percent are in such homes or any kind of institution.

Much of the fault lies with the tapes that are playing in our own heads—with retirement, we should be on the shelf. We think that we are all alike, and that when we forget a name, we have Alzheimer's. (I never could remember names, so why should I expect to remember them now?)

You have heard about the man who went to his physician, complaining about his right knee. "What do you expect at your age?" the doctor asked.

The man answered, "I expect it to work. It's the same age as my left knee, and *it* works."

In defense of modern medicine, let me add that our busy physicians deal mostly with those who are truly age-impaired, and they do not have time to deal with some of our complaints, whether real or imagined. It might help if we made lists of questions before we go.

Sometimes we who are over sixty-five hesitate to identify ourselves or to admit that we have any special needs. We are like adolescents who have a hard time finding out who they are. Who are we? Not as good any more? Not as significant? Out of the mainstream?

The truth is that we have not suddenly changed at any certain age. There is more diversity among the elderly than among younger groups. We do not change much—we just become "more so." A difficult child may become an even more difficult adult, and then a crochety old person. But most of us still have a lot of love and caring to give!

"For it is God who is at work in you, enabling you both to will and to work for his good pleasure" (Philippians 2:13). Such admonitions and promises give us power for the dream.

And so we cast aside the "handicapped" signs, at least the invisible, spiritual ones. We are not age-handicapped, we are age-challenged.

5 *Becoming Older Rather Than Old*

Underline the word *becoming.* It is akin to growing. We couldn't wait to grow up when we were children. Sometimes when we showed our immaturity, someone would shout, "Why don't you grow up?" We did. We are not children now, even when accused of entering our "second childhood." But we are children of God.

The aging John the apostle wrote: "See what love the Father has given us that we should be called children of God; and that is what we are. . . . Beloved, we are God's children now; what we will be has not yet been revealed" (1 John 3:1, 2).

When we keep the dream, we find anew that life is celebration and a gift. Christ who came to give all an abundant life is with us to guide us along the journey.

Actually, we have been getting older from the moment of birth. And medical science is adding many years to our lives. Is that good or bad? A lot depends on us and our attitudes.

Art Linkletter reminds us that *attitude* "explains what makes us act like we're forty on our seventy-fifth birthday or what makes others act and behave as though they're seventy-five on their fortieth birthday."[5]

We need the courage to grow—to grow young. Benjamin Franklin remarked some 200 years ago:

"Everybody wants to live long, but nobody wants to grow old."

I will admit that most of us do not want to use the word *old.* I still do not feel old at age seventy-six, but as physical weaknesses come, I am beginning to face reality. However, I still avoid my peers who steer every conversation to organ recitals of their ailments and a comparison of medications. I believe that when we lose our zest for life, the body turns in upon itself.

Most older adults describe their health as excellent, very good, or good, despite the fact that four out of five have at least one chronic condition such as arthritis, hypertension, heart disease, and hearing impairments.[6]

Even though physical infirmities come, plus disappointments that bring us grief, we find joy and purpose in life. As Tennyson wrote:

> Tho' much is taken, much abides, and tho'
> We are not now that strength which in old days
> Moved earth and heaven; that which we are, we are;
> One equal temper of heroic hearts,
> Made weak by time and fate, but strong in will
> To strive, to seek, to find, and not to yield.[3]

We are fortunate to be living, not in Tennyson's time, but in our age of increasing longevity. Words of the psalmist give us courage: "[The righteous] flourish in the courts of our God. In old age they still produce fruit; they are always green and full of sap" (Psalm 92:12-14).

6 Retired? Rewired? Redirected?

Full benefits of Social Security, as well as Medicare eligibility, usually begin at age sixty-five. Hence, we often think of older adulthood beginning at that time. The AARP (American Association of Retired Persons) offers membership cards at age fifty. The government, on the other hand, will likely revise the age upward.

With life expectancy increasing, retirement becomes one of the most troubling problems of old age. Some welcome it at first but then become bored. Men often feel that they have lost their identity if they are asked, "What do you do?" Women in the work force may develop the same feelings of worthlessness—unless they have been full-time homemakers, in which case they are not used to having their husbands underfoot. "I married you for better or worse, but not for lunch."

There is a whole new life for which to find a dream. Since we are concerned about the next generation, the dream may well encompass the needs of the whole world. A good example is the work of former President Jimmy Carter and his wife Rosalynn in helping establish Habitat for Humanity, and in also serving as peacemakers.

But, you say, not many of us can do anything so noble. True. We can't all be placed in the same bag, as our circumstances and talents vary so much.

Although knowing that impairment can strike at any age and that vitality can last even for the centenarian, many writers and gerontologists have tried to place retirees in at least three categories:

1) *Go-goers,* the "young old," about sixty-five to seventy-five;

2) *Slow-goers,* the "middle old," or seventy-five to eighty-five;.

3) *No-goers,* the "old old," across the age span, often victims of broken bones, strokes, and trauma. (We can add the "feeble old," homebound or in nursing homes.)

When I had the privilege a few years ago of working with older adults in a 3,000-member church, we developed a program by asking two questions: "What can we do to make life more fun for ourselves? And what can we do for others?" The most popular activity was travel, whether one-day trips or extended tours (maybe because as children of the Depression we never got to go far from home). We also developed "limited energy" excursions for the "slow-goers," such as visiting local museums. We visited our shut-in friends and neighbors, too, and sang for local nursing homes. We even had a mission work team to help as needed in camps and church institutions.

What did we call ourselves? The *Keenagers!* We became a group that was rewired and redirected. In the process, we found new friends, which is not always easy in the older years. As we traveled, we often sang:

> We're on the upward trail . . .
> Singing, singing,
> everybody singing
> as we go.

7 Connecting with God's Unfolding Dream

We can so easily lose our imagination and stop—becoming set in our ways. Or we go off on detours and become lost. Maybe we need to create new road maps in our minds.

When our four children were at home, my husband and I took them cross country on camping trips. As a busy pastor, Jim was more concerned about stretching out on the couch than in pouring over road maps and guides to campgrounds. "You tell me where to go, and I'll drive," he promised.

We had fun. But sometimes I made planning mistakes. I remember driving at dusk into a national forest, where there was supposed to be a good camping area. All that greeted us were wild animals and some shady-looking characters drinking beer on a broken down picnic table, half hidden by weeds. I lost my credibility as a navigator.

Jim had a good sense of humor, but he was half serious when he looked over the landscape and said, "I want you to know that your mother chose this place!" Our grown children still laugh about that incident as they recall our quiet ride back to the nearest small motel, about twenty miles away. Our road map had not helped us much.

I was only sixty-nine when Jim died. I asked

God to lead me through that difficult passage, or crossroad of life. I did not know which way to go, but I knew that God still had a plan for my life, and that his plan would be better than any map I could lay out for myself. The words of the apostle Paul came to me: "Now to him who by the power at work within us is able to accomplish abundantly far more than all we can ask or imagine, to him be the glory in the church and in Christ Jesus *to all generations,* forever and ever. Amen" (Ephesians 3:20-21).

On Christmas Day 1939, when England was confronted with invasion and death, King George VI quoted lines to his nation that may be of encouragement to us as we confront crises in our older years: "I said to the man who stood at the Gate of the Year, 'Give me a light that I may tread safely into the unknown.' And he replied, 'Go out into the darkness and put your hand into the Hand of God. That shall be to you better than light, and safer than a known way.' "

As we put our hands into God's hand, we connect with God's unfolding dream for us and we are able to sing:

Guide me, O Thou great Jehovah
pilgrim though this barren land.
I am weak, but thou art mighty,
hold me with thy powerful hand.
(William Williams, 1745)

8 *Going Down the Valley One-by-One*

As a child, I went with my parents to funerals of great aunts and uncles who were all quite old. I wondered why my mother cried if all were bound for heaven, as the minister said. I did not realize the great sense of loneliness that comes when a loved one has died—not until my much-loved grandfather died did grief hit me. Then I cried, at age fifteen.

I grew up and married a young student minister who soon was serving two small churches. I remember his first funeral service. The family asked me to sing a duet with Jim, which was a mistake not to be repeated. Moreover, they insisted that we sing an old gospel song, "Going Down the Valley One by One." That seemed like a morbid song to me as a young mother in my mid-twenties. To make it worse, the pianist dragged out the tempo and we sang flat, as if in a minor key. I did not like that song, and I did not understand grief.

I taught my children the traditional "Now I lay me down to sleep, I pray the Lord my soul to keep." But I did not use the ending, "If I should die before I wake. . . . " Instead, we prayed, "And guide my steps when I awake, in thine own way for Jesus' sake." Maybe not a bad idea, but I did not want to use the word "die."

Not until I reached my older years did I realize that friends and relatives are leaving me one by one. We turn first to the obituary page to find out whether anyone we know is listed. It has been said that young adults measure time since birth; older adults measure time until death.[8]

However, we are not ready to go down that valley of death. There seems to be a Creator-given drive within us to live as long as we can. The psalmist has given us a provisional time of three score years and ten (seventy years), "or perhaps eighty, if we are strong" (Psalm 90:10).

How fortunate we are to live in an age when medical science can make us "strong." The average life expectancy in the United States is seventy-six and a half years, up from forty-seven just one hundred years ago. If, in fact, a man makes it to sixty-five, his life expectancy is seventy-nine; if a woman reaches sixty-five, her life expectancy is eighty-four. And the fastest-growing segment of the population is made up of those over eighty-five.

If we beat the statistics, we have to ask ourselves, "Why am I still here?"

I will cast off childhood fears of death. I will quit using euphemisms such as "passed away" and "sleeping." Death is real; I am here by the grace of God. Life is a precious gift and I will use my last years to serve God wherever and however God leads me. I may come to hard places, but I am still on a pilgrimage.

Like the sojourner Abraham, who had been promised an inheritance, we look forward "to the city that has foundations, whose architect and builder is God" (Hebrews 11:10).

9 A New Landscape with Grief

Losses of many kinds come more often in our older years. Divorce or broken relations may hurt as much as death. We lose parents, sometimes a child or grandchild, siblings, friends, and even our pets. I don't know which is more devastating, the loss of a child or the death of a spouse. Possibly, that which causes our landscape to change most drastically is widowhood.

Did you know (according to the AARP) that the average age at which Americans are widowed is fifty-six years? That 50 percent of women over sixty-five are widows? And that in 1993 there were nearly 11 million widows and 2 million widowers? (Men die younger than woman and they tend to remarry and to marry younger women.)

Grief is real! You don't get over it, but you learn to live with it. You feel as if half of you is gone. You would not call your partner back if you could if there had been prolonged sickness or disability. (I can only imagine how great the grief when a seemingly healthy spouse meets accident or sudden death.)

But you know that only the body dies; the one you loved has gone to be with a God of love, and God still loves you. "For I am convinced that neither death, nor life, nor angels, nor rulers, nor things present, nor things to come, nor powers, nor height, nor depth, nor anything else in all creation, will be able to separate us from the love of God in Christ Jesus our Lord" (Romans 8:38-39).

Many helpful books and articles have been written about how to deal with grief. They tell us about the stages of grief, but yet no two persons grieve in the same way. The one who keeps the stiff upper lip may be hurting inside as much as the one who continuously collapses in tears.

Family and friends are helpful in getting us back on the smooth path, so long as they don't say, "Cheer up," or "I understand," when maybe they don't. As Margaret Mead said, "When a person is born, we rejoice, and when they're married, we jubilate, but when they die we try to pretend nothing happened."[1]

Something has happened, and healing does not come until we accept it. We may have many activities—friends and family to visit, some traveling to catch up on. Fine! We may stuff envelopes at our church, but mere busyness, even of the best kind, does not suffice.

Not until we get our minds off ourselves and begin to ask God for new horizons does genuine healing come. We reach out in love to other human beings. We ask God to help us see what we need to be doing. Maybe it is stuffing envelopes. In my case, it was to organize a singles dining group, as I had soon found that it was no fun to eat alone. And maybe the homebound will offer daily prayers for others—what a great service!

Whatever we do creates new landscapes for us, with some beautiful sunsets and sunrises!

10 *Angel on My Shoulder*

With fear and trembling I drove my husband Jim the 800 miles from Enid, Oklahoma, to the Mayo Clinic on June 2, 1990. He was suffering extreme heart pain and weakness. His records from successful surgeries in 1976 and 1981 were there and he was hopeful that the Clinic could help him avoid further surgery. He slept most of the way, but I thought about God's promises as the miles went by, especially Psalm 91:11, "For he will command his angels concerning you to guard you in all your ways."

After deliberating for two days, doctors decided that they must operate immediately. I was relieved when the compassionate surgeon reported that the heart bypasses, although difficult to attach, were seemingly successful. Neither he nor I could anticipate the slight stroke that Jim suffered that night. It led to swallowing difficulties, weight loss, pneumonia, and a dullness in his eyes. Even when the swallowing tubes were removed, he seldom spoke during those two long months in the hospital.

As the weeks went slowly by, our four children visited when they could. Scripture verses and hymns I had once known gave me courage to keep going back and forth to my lonely motel room. I learned that the "angel of the LORD encamps around those who fear him, and delivers them" (Psalm 34:7).

Once when I whispered in Jim's ear that he looked better, he shook his head and managed to say, "Can't walk!" The therapists thought he could learn to walk, but he did not cooperate. He repeated to me the name of his therapist friend back home.

Finally my tears came to the surface in front of the nurses, and they called a young Catholic chaplain. He listened attentively when I explained that Jim seemed to have reached a medical plateau. When I broke down, he said, "You remind me of my mother. You don't usually cry, do you?"

The understanding chaplain arranged a patient care conference for the next day. I voiced my frustration to the assembled specialists, saying, "I don't expect you to get him in perfect shape. He wants to go home." I showed them the clipping about the new rehabilitation unit in our Enid hospital.

My little angel began flying about. Soon the surgeon was making arrangements; he came to Jim's room: "Reverend White, I think you need to go home to familiar surroundings and be among those you know." We were to fly on Saturday morning, July 28, out of Rochester by single-engine charter plane with bed and a nurse and monitoring equipment.

We were packed and ready to leave at 8:30 A.M. by wheelchair cab for the airport when the charter company called: "We cannot leave as scheduled. Des Moines had a severe storm last night with 5 inches of rain. A new storm is moving in all along our line of flight. We'll call you if things change, but we would have to leave by 11:00 A.M."

"O God," I prayed, "Help me to get Jim home!"

Our patient seemed unaware of the dilemma. I was alone. I turned on the weather channel, only to hear that heavy rain and strong winds were predicted for the entire day. Old Testament pictures flashed into my mind. I prayed, "You who parted the Red Sea can make a way for us. You who led the children of Israel with clouds by day can control the clouds today."

I did not know about the prayer of Moses, who affirmed that when God "heard our voice" he sent an angel and "brought us out of Egypt" (Numbers 20:16).

The telephone roused me at 10:30 A.M. When I stumbled to the phone, I heard the welcome words: "The pilot thinks he can find his way through the clouds if you can get to the airport by 11:00 A.M. Could we ever!

An old War War II pilot confidently guided the little Beechcraft through some clouds, white and harmless. (An angel on his shoulder?) He kept in radio contact with airports along the way—Des Moines, Kansas City, Wichita, Bartlesville. Jim was comfortable and all his vital signs remained stable. I relaxed.

An unseen hand seemed to part the clouds ahead of us. Not until we were fifty miles from Enid did we see lightning and some black clouds. How, I wondered, will we get down to the airport where our ambulance was already waiting? None of us panicked. The clouds moved east just in time. We landed gently, without even a bump.

Jim was soon being rolled into the emergency room where two nurses who knew him were waiting. "Dr. White, we're so glad to see you! We've been waiting. You're home!"

He smiled and waved weakly, the last time I would see him wave. Our dedicated family doctor was also waiting, reading records and writing orders. He sent me home to rest. The night was long, but "there stood by me an angel of the God to whom I belong and whom I worship," and he said " 'Do not be afraid' " (Acts 27:23-24).

When I returned to the hospital early the next morning, nurses looked grim. I saw a moment of recognition in Jim's eyes and he seemed to smile. But suddenly, he could not squeeze my hand. A brain scan revealed that a stroke had hit his right brain, the opposite side from the one affected after surgery. The neurologist gave the word that he was brain dead, but that he would continue breathing for another five or six hours.

The children being far away, I was glad to be alone with him during those last precious hours. God was still with us! I sensed his presence near. Jim probably could not feel it as I squeezed his hand and held it. But I could whisper anyway that I loved him and softly repeat the Psalm 23. His heart kept beating steadily, but his blood pressure dropped ever so slowly. There seemed to be no pain as his breathing became slower and quietly stopped. I closed his eyes and kissed his hand. I believe there was an angel there to carry him safely Home! I experienced the peace of God's love.

11 Forever Young? Fitness and Fun

Tears of sorrow and tears of joy are not very far apart. When our "Keenagers" were getting off a bus at the church after a happy trip, some of our teenagers were amazed to see them laughing. They reported to their counselor: "Why, those old folks were having fun." Why not?

Especially after bereavement or any kind of loss, we need to pamper ourselves. Maybe go somewhere we haven't been for a long time. Or buy something we wouldn't ordinarily buy. If earthly parents enjoy giving their children good things, so does our heavenly Father like to give us good things. Maybe not always material things, but certainly spiritual things.

It is even more important to pray. In our older years, we have more time to "practice the presence" of God than ever before. I remember that when all four of our children were at home, how difficult it was to find a time for family devotions. With one preschool child, one in early elementary, one in junior high, and one in senior high, plus maybe a family night once a week—although church meetings often interfered, we were seldom together. My spiritual mentor advised me to develop my own prayer life and find time for the children individually. I wish I had followed that advice more faithfully.

Now we have more undisturbed time for ourselves. And we can regain the adventurousness of youth and listen to our own needs. This may mean changing our habits to support better health.

If we want to live longer than our parents and grandparents, we have to put on our walking shoes. Most of us are out of shape. Do not say, "It's too late for me." Many good exercises are available for muscle stretching. And best of all, the experts say, is walking. Most of us, even in the autumn of life, can still walk.

Paul said, "Athletes exercise self-control in all things; they do it to receive a perishable wreath, but we an imperishable one" (1 Corinthians 9:25).

Part of that self-control, of course, is diet. Enough said? We are bombarded with TV programs and magazine articles on what to eat and what not to eat. There is currently a daily *Senior Report* and a *Health and Wellness Report*, all giving good advice. How can we cope with so many new surveys, some of them contradictory?

Perhaps the best advice is to use moderation and common sense. Sometimes I'm tempted not to bother. My Daddy, who lived to be ninety-eight years old, ate bacon and sausage and eggs daily all his life. But maybe his carotid arteries would not have become clogged if he had known what not to eat. So, I guess I'll cut down on fat and meat; eat more vegetables, fruit and fiber; drink more water, and follow my doctor's advice.

I want to have a "young" attitude. I will have more fun if I can stay fit!

12 A Quilt: Made Up of Broken Pieces

Dad used to tease my mother about buying "material" (actually calico) and then cutting it up into tiny pieces. Grandma Maggie did not purchase fabric for her quilts. She saved all the scraps and small pieces left over after cutting out little girls' dresses and tediously patched them together. What fun it was to look at the assembled blocks and find prints from dresses that we remembered. Most brought back happy memories, a few were from sad times.

Quilts are now considered works of art. The interplay of dark and light colors in blocks of various sizes and shapes satisfies our need for beauty as we hang them on the wall or decorate our beds. But they were more than art, they were necessity to the pioneers who saved every bit of fabric to make quilts or comforters to protect against the cold of unheated bedrooms. Neighbors helped one another as they assembled for quilting bees.

During the Great Depression, Grandma and her sister-in-law spearheaded the weekly Ladies' Aid quilting at their church, giving the profit of their penny-a-yard work to missions. If a certain woman whose stitches were too long and irregular joined them, they patiently took out her stitches after she left. Nothing but the best for their church project!

Mom and her two sisters each put in a quilt almost every fall and joined each other in their homes. What fun it was to play with my cousins under those quilting frames. It was like having a playhouse with an overhead roof. Of course, our dolls listened, and so did we, to the grownup conversation. We learned who was having a baby, who was sick or near death, and who might lose their farm. Adults forgot we were there when they whispered about some wayward teenager. Broken pieces in our community were as varied as the pieces in the quilt.

As a novice, I have begun an ambitious project. At first it was to stitch and quilt a wedding quilt for each granddaughter—only four of them. But then my daughters asked, "Well, what about the boys?" Sure, I love them just as much as the girls, and their weddings are just as important. So I have ten quilts to complete before I die! (I guess I'd better have a quilting bee!)

I have a double wedding ring quilt completed for the oldest granddaughter and a triple Irish chain for the grandson whose wedding date is set. As I work, I think about each one, how their lives will be filled with sunshine and shadows, light and dark areas. I pray for each one and ask God to make me a wise grandmother.

I do believe that quilters find therapy in their work. Others find it through other crafts or hobbies. Some play cards or work crossword puzzles or make birdhouses—or write books!

It is good to find new interests and to pursue new ideas. Thus do the broken pieces of our own lives come together in beautiful patterns.

13 *Smooth the Wrinkles from My Soul*

Do you suppose that I need to find a new mirror? It's just not as clear as the ones of fifty years ago. Or maybe it's too clear. Can that really be *me?* The image doesn't look like the one I remember with dark hair and no wrinkles.

When I visited my ninety-five-year-old Aunt Kate, she asked, "Who are you?" I answered, "Marie, You know, Nettie's girl."

"Oh," she said, "I almost didn't know you with blonde hair." She was too near deaf to try to explain to her that my hair either had to be gray or blonde, and I have chosen the tinted color. One of these days, I will let it go white, because I have so many beautiful white-haired friends.

In the meantime, I will do what I can to look attractive, without paying too much attention to magazine and television ads for magic skin creams and cosmetic products. Incidentally, why is it that when a man develops wrinkles he looks "distinguished," but a woman looks "old"?

Fortunately, more good role models for the old are appearing in movies, TV drama and talk shows. The stereotypes are disappearing as attractive older people are becoming "sages," or mentors to the younger generations.

Wrinkles can easily come to our souls as well as

to our faces. Not from the exposure of too much sun, but from not enough exposure to the light of God's Word. Not enough prayer, not enough sharing of our spiritual experiences. Add to that prescription the "balm of Gilead," an aromatic ointment mentioned in the Old Testament. It is better than any skin lotion we can buy today.

Soothing words come from the old African-American spiritual:

There is a balm in Gilead
  to make the wounded whole;
There is a balm in Gilead to
  heal the sin-sick soul.

To revive the soul again, this balm is prescribed for the discouraged and those who think their life is in vain.

It might even help to smooth the wrinkles from our souls if we can get out to help someone else in church or community. When we open wide the windows of our soul, we not only receive light and a calming breeze, but God also gives us the vision of what we can be and do.

A sense of humor helps as we look at both physical and spiritual wrinkles. Stress disappears and health improves. Laughter is not all "ho, ho, ho"; it is also a quiet inner joy and peace that recreates us in both body and mind.

After all, we were created in the image of God! He loves us the way we are and guides us to dream about what we can become. Our emotional wrinkles are gone!

14 If Only! If Only!

Lot's wife got into trouble by looking back (Genesis 9:26). We may not turn into pillars of salt, but we can become very unhappy old people by continually thinking, "If only!" Being human, we cannot reach maturity without regret for some of our actions or non-actions.

I look at my four children and wonder how they could have grown into such fine adults. I made mistakes; there may be hurts in their lives of which I am not even aware. Surely the grace of God was with us.

Now as we are older, our thoughts turn more and more to family members and old friends. We wish we could do some things over again. However we do not have the past, only the present.

The cartoonist Bill Keane was sketching a *Family Circus* cartoon when little Jeffy asked, "Daddy, how do you know what to draw?"

Keane answered, "God tells me."

The little boy responded, "Then why do you keep erasing parts of it?"

The good part is that God turns our mistakes into lessons and our hurts into understanding for others. True, we do see failures of many kinds, missed opportunities and "could-have-beens"—dreams unfulfilled. Sorrows of the past sometimes return.

God gives us the way out every time we pray the Lord's Prayer: "Forgive us *as* we forgive those who sin against us." And we remember the words of Jesus: "Love your neighbor *as yourself*." First we must love and forgive ourselves. Second, as we forgive others, we can sometimes reach back to repair the places of greatest hurt.

Gail Sheehey in her latest *Passages* book, gives us much needed advice: "It's time to forgive the erring parent, embrace the estranged sibling, let go of disappointments in the prodigal child."[10]

Many of us are said to be WASPS (White, Anglo-Saxon, Protestant). We admit that we grew up in a culture where we did not say "I love you" except to our spouses—and not often enough to them. But it's not too late to express our love to those around us, to renew old relationships and build new ones, to hug a few "unhuggables."

And now, if we are lucky enough to have made adjustments in the October of life, we look forward to November with its thanksgiving time.

The apostle Paul frequently expressed his regret for his days as Saul, the persecutor of Christians. But he lived to give us an example of handling regrets and a dream to reach:

> Beloved, I do not consider that I have made it my own, but this one thing I do: forgetting what lies behind and straining forward to what lies ahead, I press on toward the goal for the prize of the heavenly call of God in Christ Jesus" (Philippians 3:13-14).

Notes, Thoughts, Prayers

Notes, Thoughts, Prayers

Notes, Thoughts, Prayers

Notes, Thoughts, Prayers

Dreams of Thanks-giving

15 "Over the River and Through the Woods"

There was no river to cross nor woods to go through on the three-mile journey to Grandpa's house. Usually it was by Model-T unless the prairie mud had not yet frozen and Dad had to hitch up the horses to the old surrey. But all of my aunts and uncles and some thirteen cousins usually made it for Thanksgiving.

The men and older boys went hunting for quail and rabbits, while we girls hurried up to the big bedroom where there were treasures awaiting—a feather bed to jump on, an old zither instrument in the corner, a china doll atop the chifferobe. On the table were stacks of school books, even some old McGuffey readers. They had belonged to Frank and Ellen and Mattie, children who had died of diphtheria in 1892. We had great fun playing school, even though our parents had warned us not to open those books. The germs might still be in the books, they thought.

Today's young parents cannot understand the fears of older generations who lived before antibiotics and the miracles of modern medicine. It was not uncommon for an epidemic to sweep through a community taking precious children from their homes. Grandma Elizabeth had kept the curls from those two little girls, and tears came as she talked about the death of Frank, the oldest. But she and Grandpa were not bitter. They gave us lessons about acceptance and gratitude "in all things."

We have all heard the admonition that we should give thanks to God our Father at all times and in everything (Ephesians 5:20). Is that possible? Maybe not completely, but God can lead us toward that goal. I learned the hard way.

In November of 1981, I struggled with the facial paralysis that is called Bell's palsy. The cause is unknown, although my doctor insisted that because it had been only six weeks since my husband Jim's first open heart surgery—even though successful—the stress I suffered had something to do with my affliction. He predicted that it would soon heal itself, but he kept having to stretch out that prediction.

When I began to recover from the shock, I was able to pen these words:

> My smile may be gone, but not my faith. Hard things come to all people. I'll admit that I feel like a little wounded sparrow, but if God's eye is on the sparrow, I know God watches me, too. After all, I could have been left in September without a husband, and so I am thankful.

Maybe the Lord sees that I need to learn some lessons in patience and understanding. I know now how stroke victims must feel when they have the sudden sensation of being helpless and their will power seems useless. In my own case, with my face all drawn to one side and unable to close my right eye, I lay awake that first restless night, feeling akin to Job and wondering how many weeks or months this might last.

But as always, when I turn to our Heavenly Father, he literally gave me songs in the night. A melody and some scattered phrases entered my consciousness. It was not until the next day that I found the song in the hymnal—"Dear Lord and Father of Mankind." The words quieted my strivings (and tossing and turning) and gave me peace:

Breathe through the pulses of desire
Thy coolness and thy balm;
Let sense be dumb, *let flesh retire;*
Speak through the earthquake, wind and fire,
O still small voice of calm.

God did not heal me instantly; in fact, I still have a bit of residual numbness. But calm and peace returned. I learned first-hand what it means to be thankful "in all things." And I am still studying lessons in patience and thanksgiving.

Now, I am trying to keep a gratitude journal, to record each day the things for which I am thankful. "Let us come into his presence with thanksgiving; let us make a joyful noise to him with songs of praise" (Psalm 95:2).

16 When the Storm Rages

Days become shorter and the sun is often hidden by clouds as we walk along life's pathway. Maybe because we are older and somewhat tired, stumbling blocks such as anxiety, sickness, sorrow, and grief appear larger than they really are. The November wind can be chilly!

Jesus and his disciples must have been very tired after a day of dealing with the multitude. Jesus asked that they cross in the boat to the other side of the lake, no doubt to seek some rest. A great windstorm arose and the boat was in danger of being swamped.

The disciples had not yet learned that to voyage with Jesus was to journey in peace, even during a storm. They cried out, "Teacher, do you not know that we are perishing?" (Mark 4:38).

We cry out, too: "Master, don't you know that I am afraid? I worry about what will happen to me, and to my loved ones. I have all these problems. . . . I am so alone. Teacher, don't you care?"

You know the rest of the story. Jesus "rebuked the wind, and said to the sea, 'Peace! Be still!' Then the wind ceased, and there was a dead calm. He said to them, 'Why are you afraid? Have you still no faith?' " (Mark 4:39-40).

In the midst of the storms of fear and anxiety, Jesus brings us peace even as he did to his disciples of long ago. When clouds appear on our horizon, he shows us the safe way to go. The sun peeks through the clouds and the rainbow of promise appears.

We remember the bold but plaintive words from a gospel song of our childhood:

Master, the tempest is raging!
The billows are tossing high!
The sky is o'er shadowed with blackness,
No shelter or hope is nigh;
"Carest thou not that we perish?"
How canst Thou lie asleep,
When each moment so madly is threat'ning
A grave in the angry deep?

But the songwriter did not stop with the questions. She proceeds to give us dramatic assurance in the chorus:

The wind and the waves shall obey my will.
Peace, be still, Peace be still! . . .
No water can swallow the ship where lies
The Master of ocean and earth and skies;
They all shall sweetly obey my will;
Peace, peace, be still!

Bring, O God, your peace to our hearts, the glory of autumn to our souls. Even when the wind blows and the waters are about to engulf our frail boats, reassure us that you are with us as a friend and guide. Amen.

17 Any Mountain Can Be Moved

Got any rivers you think are uncrossable?
Got any mountains you can't tunnel through?
God specializes in things thought impossible,
And God will do what no other power can do.

The words above made up a little chorus that we sang as teenagers. Not great poetry, but the words have proved so true.

Sometimes mountains symbolize awe-inspiring beauty, especially the western Rockies and Grand Tetons. But why would anyone want to climb them, we ask. The mountain climber answers, "Because they are there!"

We were driving the back roads from Boulder to Denver when we saw a young climber who had "frozen" halfway up a steep cliff. Frightened onlookers down below were begging him to hang on, as fear gripped us all. What a relief when the rescue squad arrived and pulled him down!

When I saw the Great Smoky Mountains just below the Cumberland Gap for the first time, I wondered how my mother's ancestors ever made it with their teams and wagons as they left their homes in Lancaster County, Pennsylvania, to claim their Revolutionary War land grants in western North Carolina (later to be called Tennessee). What kind of faith kept them going?

Once, on a plane from Tulsa to Dallas, a young

man came on board and asked for the window seat. So I took the aisle seat and promptly fell asleep. Turbulence in the air shook me awake.

My seatmate was anxiously watching the clouds. He murmured, "Winston Churchill used to say, 'There are mountains in those clouds.' "

I can't say whether the quotation was accurate, but I was surprised to hear his words. He looked like a cowboy fresh from the western plains, dressed as he was in gingham shirt, blue jeans, and boots. Seemingly well educated, he also seemed to equate mountains with danger. "Do you live in Dallas?" I asked.

"No," he answered, "I'm on my way to a bar convention in Houston." He was beginning to look relieved as we began a safe descent through the clouds. Of course he knew that planes have hit mountain peaks, but also that there were no mountains in our flight pattern.

Mountains can stand for fear and barriers and difficult roads as well as scenic beauty. Sometimes on life's journey we imagine mountains that are not there. Sometimes the mountains are real, but again Jesus reassures us: "For truly I tell you, if you have faith the size of a mustard seed, you will say to this mountain, 'Move from here to there,' and it will move; and nothing will be impossible for you" (Matthew 17:20-21).

God helps us tunnel through, go over or around, or climb down from our mountains.

18 "Who Cares?"

My son was in only about the fourth grade when he came home from school one day asking that I buy him a coat like Terry's. I knew that Terry's folks bought him anything he wanted, whether he needed it or not. And I decided that since John had a perfectly good coat, I could not grant his request. Childlike, his asking turned to begging and then demanding. I lost patience.

I had just completed a very tiring day as a first-grade substitute teacher in an inner city school where many underprivileged children were enrolled. One child's pale face haunted my memory, "John," I said, "you just don't know what it is really like to need something and not be able to get it. There was this poor little girl at school who didn't want to quit coloring when the closing bell sounded. I told her that she could take her half-completed picture home and finish it there. Do you know what the child answered? It was 'I can't. I don't have any color crayons at home, and my mother won't get me any.'"

John had a ready answer: "So...who wants crayons?"

It's impossible for a child who has always had crayons to put himself in the place of one who hasn't. Who cares?

I wonder whether God our Father sometimes

loses patience with our indifference and selfishness. We have so many wants of our own—wants that sometimes increase as we grow older. We fail to see those about us who have so many needs. I am convinced that when we try to meet those needs, as God lays them on our hearts, we help ourselves as well as others.

By contrast, when our thoughts are turned in upon ourselves, we develop more problems, even physical ailments. Then we really feel sorry for ourselves.

Do you know who most of the volunteers were when I helped organize a visitors' group in our church to keep in touch with the disabled and elderly? Not the younger people, and not the traveling Keenagers, but those who were themselves in their November years. Emma, for example, at age eighty, was rather crippled with arthritis, but she always managed to get to our monthly meetings. She could report that she had visited her assigned shut-ins, and that she had also kept in touch with them by telephone. What's more, she often brought her delicious cream puffs to share with the rest of us! She was a very caring person.

God is not through with us yet. The promise is this: "For it is God who is at work in you, enabling you both to will and to work for his good pleasure" (Philippians 2:13).

Because God cares, we care!

19 Age 120: Science-Fiction Dream or Nightmare?

We are all growing older, but what if we get too old? Possibility or problem? How do we feel about it?

My friend Nina was celebrating her sixtieth birthday, saying, "I'm only middle-aged. That means I'll live to be 120. So?"

Maybe this vibrant, happy woman was not far from reality. Some scientists are now saying that our bodies are made to last a life span of 120 years. Of course, our life expectancy is far less; we won't all make it, but some will. We see Willard Scott on TV showing pictures of those past 100, each with a different so-called secret for success.

A few years ago I attended a prayer and Bible conference where I took part in a workshop entitled "The Spiritual Call of Later Life." Doctor Jane Tibault, the capable young psychologist who was our leader, asked our group of mostly middle-aged participants how we felt about getting older. "How many would be happy to reach 120? How many would not? And why?"

We raised our hands to vote; with half willing to become 120, the others not. Various reasons were given. I am sorry to say that I voted no. I have always said I would like to live as long as I can, provided my body doesn't outlive my mind. But on that particular day I was feeling sad for my father, then ninety-six and in a nursing home. I do not think he had Alzheimer's, since he was quite lucid most of the day. But sometimes he did not know where he was when he first awakened. In fact, he occasionally got up early, dressed himself, and put on his hat. When the nurse stopped him, he was angry; "I have to go empty the combine and take a load of soybeans to the elevator."

Dad may have had too much sedation; and he suffered some depression from the loss of my mother and others whom he had loved. Increasingly, when I visited he would say, "I don't know why I'm still here. I have a better place than this to go." He had another two years to wait, but yet he had some moments of joy.

Surely, Dr. Tibault was right—old people are God's gift to the world. God may say to us, "I need you . . . and your wisdom." Our goal is then to be able to say, "To me, living is Christ and dying is gain" (Philippians 1:21).

We live in a society without hope and afraid of suffering. We have Dr. Kevorkian and a growing debate over physician-assisted suicide. I do not have the answer, but surely there is a difference between allowing a patient to die naturally and artificially prolonging life. Life is a gift and should be treated as such at any age.

My husband, Lance, wanted so much to live as long as he could, but in the end, because of congestive heart failure, he became part of the hospice program, content to die in our own home. He underlined the words: "For we know that if the earthly tent we live in is destroyed, we have a building from God, a house not made with hands, eternal in the heavens" (2 Corinthians 5:1). Surely he is in that house now, along with my dad.

20 Between Memory and Hope

"We always move between memories and hope." I don't know who said it, but it's true. Out of the past comes renewed hope and dreams for the future.

As we pause to stand upon the mountain peak of time, we look back to live again the happy experiences of our childhood, youth, young adult, and middle years. Some kind of spiritual anesthesia seems to erase the unhappy times and lost opportunities, especially if we have been able to forgive ourselves and others. We become collectors—events of joy, friendships remembered, and dreams come true. Our minds are happily peopled now with two or three generations of those who exist only in memory.

We think more and more about our children or others important to us. Grandchildren and other young people may ask what it was like in the "good old days." Let's tell them our life stories and also the lessons we have learned.

Several years ago I began to write my autobiography in bits and pieces. Those pieces may never come together, but at least they can clutter my children's attics, along with scrapbook material from their growing-up years. My theme will be "With a Song in My Heart." I want my descendants to know that my life has been happy even in the midst of adversity. They do not know what life was like during the Great Depression or during the wars that followed, all before television and computers. I can tell them about their ancestors, their roots. Hopefully, I can teach them lessons about work and money, love and marriage. Above all, I want them to know that "all things work together for good for them that love God" (Romans 8:28).

If I become too feeble to write or type, maybe I can ask them to gather up their questions so that I can try to answer them on tape. They might even videotape me!

I am reminded of the psalmist's prayer:

O God, from my youth you have taught me,
  and I still proclaim your wondrous deeds.
So even to old age and gray hairs,
  O, God, do not forsake me,
until I *proclaim* your might
  to all the generations to come.
(Psalm 71:17-18)

However, I am also reminded that we must not let yesterday take up too much of today, that, as much as we treasure memories, we cannot become their prisoners. Our hope still lies in the future.

And so, on our mountaintop, we turn 180 degrees to the right. We are going forward now, to possess a new land and to make some new memories. Hope increases as we dream new dreams, dreams of sharing whatever wisdom we may have acquired,

This is the day of new beginnings,
  time to remember and move on....

21 *To Love Again?*

Do you miss the love and companionship that came with a long and happy marriage? Maybe your memories are sufficient to keep you going. But maybe God has a new partner for you.

If an earlier marriage ended in bitterness or divorce, remember that God is a God of forgiveness and of new beginnings. God may have a surprise for you. Second marriages come after both divorce and death.

Lance Webb and I had only four and a half years together, but I would not have missed that precious time with him. Our marriage came only one year after losing our long-time spouses, Elizabeth and Jim, in death. Our friendship had existed for twenty-five years, going back in time to the period of Illinois Methodism when he had been the bishop who chose my Jim as his first district superintendent. But we had not seen each other for several years—not until we each reached out to try to console the other.

Our first steps were awkward—we later chuckled as we said that Jim and Elizabeth must have been "up there" laughing at us. Feelings of disloyalty and guilt vanished as Lance remembered how Elizabeth had admonished him that he must find another wife if she died first, and as I discovered Jim's writings saying that after his death, I must find a new love.

Our courtship was brief, because we wanted to seek what happiness we could together; we realized that at ages seventy and eighty-one our married years might be few. And so our wedding took place on June 22, 1991, with all seven children and their spouses, fifteen grandchildren, and one great-grandchild standing along the altar rail as witnesses. We were all smiles, but as I repeated the vow "in sickness and in health," a sudden icy premonition punctured my heart.

Lance was unaware of this fear. In fact, the next day before we left the hotel room, he wrote in his journal: "Dear Lord, on this first morning of our new life together, we wait in humble awe and thanksgiving as we look back over the cold and dark winter of our grief. . . . The time of the singing of the turtle dove has come. . . . As we have shared our love physically, our hearts and souls are united not only to love each other but also to open a channel for your love to flow to others. We trust you to be with us. Amen."[1]

God truly was with us, in spite of many adjustments due to ill health. A valve was successfully placed in Lance's heart less than one year later; he recovered but then gradually became weaker.

The last time he drove a car was on my birthday, March 28, 1994. He insisted on going to a large drug store to buy me a card and gift. He forgot that he had driven my blue car and so could not find his white one in the parking lot. After the police had searched the parking lot in vain, they called me. I hopped into the "stolen" car and immediately spotted the one he had driven.

We laughed about the episode, glad that it had turned out well. He wrote on my birthday card this beautiful message:

> To My dearest Marie,
>
> As we close the most unusual birthday celebration—as I went to get this card and thought our Skylark was stolen when all of the time I was driving the other car! And you came! May this remind us that always when bad things happen there will always be a good ending—not as good as this one, but *always God will bring us through.* In some way God's will enables "all things to work together for good."
>
> Our nearly three years as partners in marriage and in our living have been filled with difficult, costly, but wonderful times. You are a miracle sent of God. I love you more each day. Your joyful, self-giving love is precious indeed!
>
> So we end this your 73rd birthday with a good laugh about the car that wasn't stolen.
>
> With Agape Love,
> Lance

I lost this wonderful and sensitive man just eighteen months later, but that is another story.

Just now, I want to add a bit of advice to the widowed or divorced who are considering marriage. You need a sense of humor as you make adjustments in longtime life styles. Laugh at failing memories and little mistakes before they become earth-shaking. Admit your own shortcomings and overlook your partner's. Age should give stability and the ability to manage emotions.

Are you affectionate when together? Have you discussed the place of romance in your new life? You may be getting older, but you are still sexual beings. Talk about expectations and physical needs. If cuddling is sufficient for one, that's OK if it pleases the other. Don't expect too much—or too little! Love can be tender and intimate at any age. And above all, make no comparisons with a former mate.

Be practical in another way: Make a premarital agreement after talking to your attorneys. Report this to your children. It will help them accept the new stepparent when they realize you are not marrying for money.

Are you marrying for love? Not because you need a cook or housekeeper, or a chauffeur or business manager? You are lonely now, but can you really let someone take away part of your independence? Love can and will be costly, but I think it's worth it. Above all, pray about your decisions, heeding the ageless advice of the apostle Paul:

> Love is patient; love is kind; love is not envious or boastful or arrogant or rude. It does not insist on its own way; it is not irritable or resentful; it does not rejoice in wrongdoing, but rejoices in the truth. It bears all things, believes all things, hopes all things, endures all things.
>
> *Love never ends.*
>
> (1 Corinthians 13:4-8)

22 *Don't Make Me Laugh!*

Sarah was ninety years old and Abraham was 100 years of age when the angels appeared with their unbelievable promise. Sarah stood inside the tent laughing. I would have laughed too at being told that I would conceive and bear a child. At first she denied her laughter, but after the promised son had indeed been born, her laughter changed to joy. Sarah said, "God has brought laughter for me; everyone who hears will laugh with me" (Genesis 21:6).

Some of my peers are much younger than Sarah, but they no longer laugh at anything. They look as if their faces would crack if a faint smile turned into joyous laughter. Don't they know that God's promises apply to them? Fortunately, the promises are not to bear children in old age, although some brave parents today are bravely struggling to rear grandbabies. Regardless of circumstances, God's promises are still valid and God's joy is meant for us.

Can't you just see a circle of laughing children, clasping hands and singing, "Here We Go 'Round the Mulberry Bush," or some such song? We as older children can join hands and sing with all creation.

This is my father's world. O let me ne'er forget
that though the wrong seems oft so strong,
God is the ruler yet.

This is my Father's world. Why should my heart be sad?
The Lord is king; let the heavens ring!
God reigns, let the earth be glad.
(Maltbie D. Babcock, 1901)

Before Jesus called the little children to him, he must have enjoyed seeing them at play. Play is not for children only. I wonder what Jesus thinks of us. Surely we do not laugh enough—we do not play enough.

Play might be defined as doing something you don't have to do, just for the fun of doing it. Too often, we really want to do something, but we say, "I'm too old for that," just as Sarah did. And because we don't believe God's promises, we miss out on laughter.

Art Linkletter, who himself brought laughter to many, tells about fascinating "Senior Americans," among whom was Lowell Thomas. After losing his wife of sixty years, Thomas remarried in his eighties. He set off for a honeymoon around the world. "I wired him," said Linkletter, "in Hong Kong at the Mandarin Hotel: 'Lowell, I have great faith in your strength and virility, but a honeymoon like this could be fatal.' "

Thomas wired back to his friend, "If she's got to go, she's got to go."[1]

No wonder that Gail Sheehy in her latest book, *New Passages,* describes the eighties as the "Uninhibited Eighties."[2]

Sometimes we need to day dream as well as to dream, to let the little child inside of us come out to play, to let go of the world with its cares.

23 *Why Worry?*

Lance used to tease me about frequently saying, "Things will work out." Of course he knew that things do not always work out the way we want, but that things do work together for good.

God had given me my first lesson about the futility of worry when I was only thirty-three years old. I had a three-month-old son, an older little cowboy who called himself Stevie Roy Rogers (difficult to corral!), and two daughters already very much involved in school and their own activities. I wanted to see them all grow up.

A lump had developed near the base of my neck that I assumed was just a thyroid enlargement. But when my doctor saw it, he was alarmed; he said that it was a nodule on my lymph gland and that after Christmas I should enter the hospital for tests. The medical books told me that it could be the first symptom of leukemia or of cancer of the lymph glands. What's more, we had no medical insurance at that time.

I worried! I was not afraid for myself—I had faced death once before. But I could just imagine well-meaning acquaintances saying, "Poor Brother White! He was such a capable young minister and now burdened with an invalid wife, he has to spend most of his time doing housework. His children look like last year's rummage sale, and they aren't taking music lessons any more. The parsonage is a wreck. . . ."

After a week of midnight tossing and turning, I began to turn to the Scripture and prayer. Nothing dramatic happened; newfound peace came very gradually. Bible verses that I had learned in childhood took a new meaning until finally I was able to place not only myself but also my family in God's hand. By the time New Year's Day arrived, I could sing, "My times are in thy hand."

When I returned to the doctor, that little lump had begun to shrink; another week, and it was almost gone. My conscientious doctor smiled in a relieved sort of way, telling me I could forget about it.

Although I've had to relearn that lesson several times, I have a bit of scribbling to serve as a reminder. During a night when I had been unable to sleep (just before Christmas when the children were all asleep), I wrote these words:

"I sought the Lord, and he heard me
  and delivered me from all my fears" (Psalm 34:4).
If I should *die,* O God,
  please do not call it death;
'tis but a passing to a life where I may grow faster
  and learn more than has been permitted here.
My only fear
  is for the future of my loved ones;
I pray that they grieve not,
  but dedicate themselves to the service
    of God and all mankind—
And I shall be immortal through their lives.

As for me, I will have had thirty-three years,
As much as the Master himself
had here on earth....

"For to me living is Christ,
and dying is gain" (Philippians 1:21).
If I may live yet many years,
even as did John the disciple of old,
Then let me face life
with a new determination:
May I keep my values straight
and see life through the eyes of God.
May I practice God's presence,
not occasionally, but daily.
May I give freely, knowing that
her to whom much is given
of her shall much be required.
I want my life to grow greater and wiser,
"For now I know only in part:
then I will know fully, even as I have been fully known.
And now faith, hope, and love abide, these three;
and the greatest of these is love"
(1 Corinthians 13:13).

What a prescription for life I had given myself! I was able that night to go back to bed and sleep peacefully. Worry was gone.

I had found my dream of usefulness, to try to love as God does and to try to see life through God's eyes. To try to commit my life totally to God. Of course, I have failed many times. But now that I am old, that dream continues to this day.

24 *Keep Moving...*

Jim's old Granddad Kerr was an immigrant who never lost his broad Scottish brogue or his love of life. At age ninety his skinny frame could be spotted as he jauntily walked with his cane down the street. When his grandsons began to acquire their first jalopies, they would frequently pull alongside and ask, "Grandpop, do you want a ride?"

Always he would wave them away with his cane, "Awaye we' ye, laddie, I'm in a hurry." That spirit doubtless helped him live so long—he kept moving.

To use another family illustration, we think my mother might have lived a few years longer if she had continued to lead a more active life. When she was only sixty-three, she had gall bladder surgery. Although she recovered physically, she quit doing things. Dad ran the vacuum cleaner and treated her as if she were a semi-invalid. He discouraged her from working outside among her flowers. She began to doze more and more in her easy chair, even during "As the World Turns."

Perhaps it was her inactivity that led to several ministrokes (TIAs) during her early seventies and finally to the major stroke that made her an invalid for two-and-a-half years. Dad lovingly cared for her in their home, refusing to put her in a nursing home. He did not realize then—and neither did I—

that a rehabilitation center with trained therapists might have helped her learn to walk again.

Like everyone else, I think about my heredity and what may happen to me. When I passed most of my physical with flying colors (meaning chiefly that blood pressure and cholesterol count were lower), I was very grateful. But I complained to the doctor that my leg muscles are just not as strong as they should be. He asked, "Do you walk each day?"

"Well, when the weather is good and if I feel like it."

He stopped me. "I want you to walk every day—well, maybe not on Sunday—without fail. The reason George Burns has kept so active is that he walks. He keeps moving." (I know that Burns has since died, but he lived to be 100.)

My doctor pursued his lecture. "Do you have any steps to climb?"

"Yes, there are two levels to my house."

"Well, climb them. And do you have any hills you can walk up?"

I laughed. I live in the hills. It is at least one-fourth mile uphill to my mailbox, but I did not confess that I often jump into the car to drive up to it.

It won't be easy to change my ways, but I guess I had better try if I want to live as long as old Grandpa Kerr. I know that an aging body inevitably loses some of its ability. But I also know that I can find new and exciting ways to live if I keep moving.

Our longevity may not be determined so much by our genes as by our attitude. For in God "we live and move and have our being. . . . For we too are his offspring" (Acts 17:28).

25 Making a List and Checking It Twice

Judging from the jokes we often tell on ourselves, most of us at some point feel that we are "losing our marbles." That's how it is when I go downstairs to get something but then can't remember what I went down for. I drove to the post office to take a letter, but I forget to take the letter with me. Or I let the teakettle boil dry on the burner—a friend says she has lost three kettles that way.

It's really not funny, but it does us good to laugh at ourselves. We say that our "get up and go has got up and went" or "I don't mind getting old, but I do miss my mind."

One problem that drives many of us to assisted living is medication. The kitchen or bathroom counter has accumulated bottles of pills, plus hearing aids, dentures, and strong eyeglasses. How easy at bedtime to wonder, "Did I take this pill, or was it that pill?"

Wisely, we avoid asking for pills that can be harmful if taken in combination with other drugs. We keep our internist informed about prescriptions from other physicians. Too many of our contemporaries are taking sleeping pills, and who knows what—no wonder they move like zombies! They would be shocked if we told them that they suffer from drug addiction.

Nonetheless, there are some medicines that I

must take each day. I line up the day's allotment as soon as I get up each morning. If they're gone at bedtime, I know that I've remembered.

I also make more lists than I used to. I may not believe in Santa Claus, but I do believe that "making a list and checking it twice" will help me get through the months of November and December. My calendar is filled with upcoming events that I might otherwise forget.

The brain, medical science tells us, is a muscle. Brain cells are stimulated by use, just as are our other muscles. We "use it or lose it." Some brain cells may die, but the brain keeps growing if it is stimulated through meditation and lifelong learning. And so we keep reading, keep writing, keep balancing checkbooks as long as we can. We can exercise our mind and soul as well as our body!

When I can't give answers quickly to questions, it must be "computer overload." When I can't remember a person's name, if I relax for a second the name comes. I remind myself that I can still learn new things, my reasoning is not impaired, and I have valuable experience to serve as back-up to solutions. I stop myself if I start to say, "I'm too old."

I was fifty when I taught myself to type; then I learned—ever so slowly—to use the word processor. I may sign up for a computer course in our community college. Some of my friends are studying new languages, learning to paint or to play musical instruments.

Surely the Master Teacher would say to us: "Make a list of what you want to do. Be a risk-taker. Go for it!" God is not through with us yet.

26 "I've Paid My Dues!"

If they were carrying the Olympic torch through your neighborhood, would you line up to carry it? Or would you even line up, saying instead, "Let others do it!" I wonder what I would do.

It would be so easy to retire to the rocking chair and sleep the rest of my life away. "I've done my share. Don't bother me now." But God nudges me awake. God still has work for me to do, even in the November of my life. There is a world out there, hurting and in need of my witness to the truth.

Jeremiah promised the children of Israel in exile that after seventy years they would return to Jerusalem. He added these words of assurance: "For surely I know the plans I have for you, says the LORD, plans for your welfare and not for harm, to give you a future with hope" (Jeremiah 29:11). God has some plans for us, too.

I'm sorry to admit it, but sometimes the church does not include us in its plans. When we reach a certain age, a few capable people are made "honorary" to make room for younger leaders. That is understandable, and yet we need the wisdom of the aged along with the enthusiasm of the young.

I remember "Ralph," a retired banker in a certain church. When an expensive building project came up, board members said, "Let's just borrow from ourselves. We can get the money out of the trust fund and pay it back later."

Ralph said, "No, it may be legal, but it is not wise." They did it anyway, and now, twenty years later, they are still paying it back. The old man was right.

On the other hand, sometimes older individuals do not know when to pass on the torch. There was the ninety-year-old woman who insisted on teaching a Sunday school class even though she no longer prepared for it and would tell the same stories over and over. She could have served in other ways.

I remember another ninety-year-old whom we called "Aunt Nan," a bedfast woman, but with such a sweet spirit that college students in the small town beat a path to her door. She prayed for each one by name and was a blessing to all who knew her.

The secret may be to discern how we fit into God's plan. As we find the volunteer opportunities for which we are suited, we help not only ourselves but also our churches and communities.

It's not easy for the young to look beyond the wrinkles and see the real persons that we are. But the world is still full of surprises for those who continue to give with a smile. And so we sing:

> O Jesus, I have promised to serve thee to the end;
> be thou forever near me, my Master and my friend.
> I shall not fear the battle if thou art by my side,
> nor wander from the pathway if thou wilt be my guide.
>
> (John E. Bode, 1866)

27 *Fight the Good Fight*

Paul was very near the end of his earthly life, much nearer than most of us are, when he said to the young Timothy: "I have fought the good fight, I have finished the race, I have kept the faith" (2 Timothy 4:7).

The apostle may have been thinking about the Olympic games, the great games of ancient Greece that required months of training and a pledge to keep the rules of honor. If so, he was saying, "I have kept the rules: I have played the game."

Or, of more importance, he may have been saying, "I have kept my faith: I have never lost my confidence and my hope."[1]

What are we saying to the young men and women of today? We like to tell them stories about how hard we had it "away-back-when." Of course some of the stories are true. My father's generation fought in a war "to make the world safe for democracy." My generation fought in World War II and the undeclared Korean conflict, to defeat the forces of evil that challenged us.

But then we entered a time of complacency and struggle for riches. Maybe we didn't really teach our baby boomers the values in which we believed. Be that as it may, our world now faces an unprecedented number of social issues. We must overcome our old prejudices and "lay aside every weight"—even the weight of our infirmities—and continue to "run with perseverance the race that is set before us" (Hebrews 12:1).

We have to be part of our changing world community. Our weakness is that we hate change; that attitude leads to noninvolvement. We go to sleep on the sidelines when we should be participants, contributors, and counselors. A side benefit: There is surely no better prescription for the discouragement and depression of old age than to get involved.

Our churches need us to provide a matured faith. Our country needs us to help find answers to so many social problems: national and international drug abuse and crime, terrorism, minority injustices, health care for all (including long-term care), abuse of both young and old, educational inequalities, displaced persons, influence of the media, euthanasia, and attention to our environment for the sake of our grandchildren. The list goes on and on, but we need not be intimidated if we each choose just one issue in which we can make a difference.

We are not out of the race. We remember Queen Esther, who was willing to sacrifice her life for her people. She acted bravely after being challenged, Who knows whether you have not come to the kingdom "for just such a time as this?" (Esther 4:14).

Like Paul, we will attempt to fight the good fight, complete the race, and keep the faith.

28 Tomorrow Is a Dream That Leads Me Onward

Robert Browning is often quoted for his words:

Grow old along with me!
The best is yet to be,
The last of life, for which the first was made,
Our times are in his hand.[1]

Older adults in the autumn of life may well make a question of Browning's lines: Is the best really yet to be? Is life like a glass that's half empty, or is it half full? Time is short for everyone. Even today's young adults will have left the scene before the new century ends. Human nature makes us protest.

Dylan Thomas raged against "the dying of the light." He cried,

Do not go gentle into that good night,
. . . .
Old age should burn and rave at close of day.[2]

But we know that old age is not some strange and unnatural part of life, even though we have to accept its limitations. A continued commitment to the God who gives us life leads us onward. To live happily, to live at all, requires purpose and determination.

Phillip L. Berman, in his excellent book *The Courage to Grow Old,* edited the contributions of forty older people. The essays are arranged in chronological order, from the youngest (born in 1922) to the oldest (born in 1897). He notes that as you read further you find more renunciation and contentment. Those in their eighties and nineties are most willing to reflect on the past and the "prospect of death." Not all of the writers have a great faith in God, although most do. But the common wisdom is that we must live creatively to the end.[3] In other words, we all need a dream.

I have kept copies of our Keenage newsletter captioned, rightly or wrongly, "Our Best Years." In the autumn 1987 issue, I find one little verse (author unknown) that puts our dream in every day language:

> Get up in the morning, look in the mirror
> and say "Hi . . . I like you."
> Thank God for another day and all it problems,
> surprises and joy.
> For problems; remember that the good Lord
> never put burdens on shoulders not strong
> enough to bear them.
> The world is full of surprises; they are the
> oils of the machinery of living. . . .
> Joy is not receiving, but giving with one's
> smile, in word, deed and thought.

We can be sure that God has some unexpected discoveries, surprises, and joys ahead of us if we let God lead us forward—even to the gates of heaven.

Notes, Thoughts, Prayers

Notes, Thoughts, Prayers

Notes, Thoughts, Prayers

Dreams of Peace

29 *En Route on the Christmas Journey*

December begins with Advent and closes during the twelve days of Christmas. January 6 is sometimes observed as the anniversary of the Wise Men's appearance after they had journeyed to find Jesus. Whatever the date, we know that they did stop first in Bethlehem —perhaps lost and discouraged, or why else would they have inquired of Herod?

We, too, at whatever age, are called to make a "journey to Jesus." We pray that we, too, may be inspired by the mystery and majesty of the sky, but able to avoid dangers such as the Wise Men encountered in Herod. We are "overwhelmed with joy" as we find the Christ, and we kneel before him and offer him the gift of our lives.

The wise men did not stay in Bethlehem nor return to Herod's Jerusalem, but they "left for their own country by another road" (Matthew 2:12).

We go forward on our own roads until we reach our Father's house. We hear again the promise of Jesus: "In my Father's house there are many dwelling places. . . . I go to prepare a place for you." There may be trials and pain on the road, but Jesus comforts us: "So you have pain now; but I will see you again and your hearts will rejoice, and no one will take your joy from you" (John 14:2; 16:22). Thus it is that a sense of peace and contentment comes.

Why is it then that we so often deny the reality of death? In our youth-worshiping society, we look at death as just another disease to be conquered. But it is a certainty; it is not an option. If we live past our allotted years, we are here by the grace of God.

Elisabeth Kübler-Ross, a modern writer who has studied death and dying at length, reminds and challenges us: "It's not really the dying that's so hard; dying takes no skill and no understanding. It can be done by anyone. What is hard is living—living until you die, whether your death is imminent or a long way off; whether it's you who are dying or one you love."[1]

> Christians are not immune to the fear of death. There is a mystery about death that even the wisest person cannot understand. But we do know that since neither life nor death can separate us from the love of God, our relationship with God will not end with death. A risk greater than the fear of dying is the risk of not living to the full.
>
> Like the wise men, we sometimes have trouble finding our way. But we, too, can kneel before the Christ to give him the years of our lives. He in turn offers us the gifts of faith, hope, and love—gifts that enable us to live fully until we die.

We will reach the end of our journey with the excitement of a child who is anticipating Christmas. Some days may be long, but Christmas will come! The star will guide us to the "perfect light." We have a way yet to go. . . .

30 *Valley of the Shadow*

Since I am one who fits the category of "old," my granddaughter asked to interview me. It was for a graduate psychology course at Northwestern University. The students had compiled a list of questions, mostly about how it "used to be." Finding it fun to talk about our early years, we were both laughing.

Then Jill grew serious as she asked me the last question: "Are you afraid to die?"

"No," I answered softly, "I'm not."

Jill seemed surprised as she looked at me intently. "Well, why not? Most of us in the class are afraid."

My feelings were not easy to put into words, but I knew that I had faced death several times in my life and had conquered my fear. After a moment, I tried to explain, "I sat by your grandfather Jim's bedside while he was dying, and I also watched your step-grandfather Lance die. I can't explain it, but a wonderful peace seemed to come over their faces. We felt God's presence. It was a good experience, one to be treasured. We don't need to be afraid!"

It is human nature to be afraid of the unknown. Only with maturing faith in God do we conquer that fear. I recall that as a child I was afraid that I might suddenly die with some unforgiven sin—like maybe after a quarrel with a friend. Now I know that God is like a loving parent who does not disown a child but lifts her up after she stumbles and falls. God's love is very real, and is never withdrawn from us. We are saved not by our goodness, but by God's grace.

I should have told Jill about times in my own life, such as when I was facing childbirth or surgery, that I remained unafraid. How? I simply repeated the words of Psalm 23 to myself, entrusting myself to God's care. Then as I went under anesthesia, I could calmly envision green pastures, the still waters, the paths alongside the streams. I could lift my eyes to the Good Shepherd: "Even though I walk through the valley, I will fear no evil; for you are with me. . . . Surely goodness and mercy shall follow me all the days of my life: and I will dwell in the house of the LORD my whole life long" (Psalm 23:4, 6).

Usually when we are called to go "through the valley," we come through it to find that we are still on our earthly pilgrimage. We have simply become more certain that the Shepherd with his staff is walking with us.

However, as we grow older we are aware that there is a valley at the end of life that does lead to the house where there are many rooms prepared for us. And so, it is not morbid to talk about death—it can be reassuring.

I wonder why should we not prepare for this final event of our earthly life even as we prepared for earlier events, or "passages," in our lives?

31 "Life Is Like a Box of Chocolates"

Forest Gump said about boxed chocolate candies, "You never know what you will get." Surely not the marshmallow or maraschino cherry chocolates that my kids used to pinch and leave in the box. (Finally I had to make a rule: You pinch it, you take it or you do not get another one. They wanted the caramel and nut-filled chocolates.)

Life is like that. We older adults have more comfort, more independence, more material goods than any generation before us. In addition, we have the best medical care in the world.

We also get some things we don't want. We don't like what is happening to our bodies, maybe even to our minds. Our powers of going and doing decline. We are concerned that we may become a burden to others. We dread the day when we may have to give up our drivers' licenses. We lose a certain amount of independence. And we fear that we may have to leave our homes or apartments to enter nursing homes, where some of our friends are already living.

There is no way to prevent some things. We resist change, wanting everything the way it was. Even our best-laid plans do not always work out. We wish that we could choose from the box of chocolates only those that we want and discard the others.

We learn that there is no answer to "why me,

Lord?" Jesus has to remind us that our Heavenly Father "makes the sun to rise on the evil and on the good, and sends rain on the righteous and on the unrighteous" (Matthew 5:45).

Most devastating of all is the loss of loved ones, lifelong friends and confidants, the people with whom we could say, "Remember when?" We shared many happy times together. After they leave us, it is not easy to make new friends—casual friends, yes; but confidants, no.

We often see this verse on sympathy cards:

God has not promised skies always blue,
Flower-strewn pathways all our lives through.
God has not promised sun without rain,
Joy without sorrow, peace without pain.

But God has promised strength for the day,
Rest for the labor, light for the way,
Grace for the trials, help from above,
Unfailing sympathy, undying love.

(Author unknown)

If we can look with the eyes of faith, claiming God's promises, then we can take what comes at this moment in time. We face each day with courage, content to let be what will be. And God gives us the power to dream about tomorrow.

32 *How Firm a Foundation*

When Paul wrote to the young Timothy about true riches, he added lines about those who store up "the treasures of a good *foundation* for the future, so that they may take hold of the life that is really life" (1 Timothy 6:19).

Isn't that what we want, life that is really life, both abundant and eternal, that begins here on earth? I discovered a firm foundation when I gave my heart to Christ many years ago. But my feet were in danger of slipping off that rock during the summer of 1995 when I cared for Lance under the hospice program in our home. It was a joy to be with him, but like many volunteer caregivers, I suspect, I felt so confined. No place to go except for groceries, no meetings—church or community—to attend, no visits to friends or relatives (who were all far away).

I was lonely and somewhat depressed. Most of all, I was concerned about what might lie ahead. We had not been able to attend church for a few weeks due to Lance's increasing weakness. But then one Sunday in August, he surprised me. "Marie," he said, "I think I could get down the aisle with my walker if we could go to that new little handicapped-accessible church." Neither of us realized that it would be his last time.

The worship service was uplifting for both of us. I don't remember the sermon, but I do recall the assurance and hope that came quite unexpectedly when we joined to sing:

"Fear not, I am with thee, O be not dismayed,
for I am thy God and will still give thee aid;
I'll strengthen and help thee, and cause thee to
stand
upheld by my righteous, omnipotent hand.
When through the deep waters I call thee to go,
the rivers of woe shall not thee overflow;
for I will be with thee, thy troubles to bless,
and sanctify to thee thy deepest distress."

You have recognized the hymn, "How Firm a Foundation," based on Isaiah 43:1-2. As we remained seated to sing, Lance reached for my hand and smiled at me. I thanked God that even though we were passing through deep waters, God was still with us. Later that day, I recorded my short prayer: "Thank you, O God, for putting the song back in my heart. We will come through this with your help."

Now I join in prayer with all those who are care-givers for loved ones. I think about "Mary," who watches over her husband with Alzheimer's in their home. He is not able to recall her name, let alone squeeze her hand. Occasionally she gets out, thanks to friends and relatives. She is grateful for nurses who come to supervise his care.

Surely there must be a special place in heaven for those who suffer with Alzheimer's and other chronic illnesses. To care for them is truly giving up one's life for another.

33 *"Set Your House in Order"*

I wonder what Hezekiah, the good king of Old Testament times, did when Isaiah commanded him: "Set your house in order, for you shall die" (2 Kings 20:1). Sometimes you and I fail to put our "house in order" because we have confidence in our would-be heirs, not realizing that they will be bound by the laws of the state when we die.

It became necessary for me to make a new will, simple though it is, each time I moved from one state to another—Illinois, Oklahoma, Texas, and now Arkansas. To my surprise, I learned that in my new state it is legal to file with my will a handwritten list of who is to receive each piece of memorabilia and personal property. What a good idea, I thought, because I have seen families torn apart over who gets a piece of costume jewelry or grandfather's clock.

But when I asked my children to make known what they would like, all four evaded the request. They did not want to talk about it—denial, I guess. So I will give them some things here and now, and make my list without their assistance.

Your lawyer and family doctor are the best persons to help you plan for the unknown future. In addition, much good literature is available through the AARP, Social Security Administration, and agencies for the aging. You need to make decisions about making a will or creating a living trust and who will be the administrator or executor. Let that person know where your important papers are located.

Then there is the problem of powers of attorney for health and also living wills. To protect ourselves and to help our loved ones in future difficult decisions, we should give someone legal right to make choices for us if we become unconscious or otherwise unable to make them for ourselves. If we postpone our decisions, which is so easy to do, the state may have to intervene and appoint a guardian for us.

We can also in a legal document, after discussion with family, direct our doctors as to how much medical treatment we want or do not want if we cannot speak for ourselves. Would we, for instance, want CPR (cardiopulmonary resuscitation), a respirator if we cannot breathe for ourselves, artificial nutrition as by a stomach tube, and other life-prolonging treatments if we should become terminally ill?

Also, how do we feel about organ donation, or about cremation? So many questions and decisions face us in our modern world. We have to plan for the realities of life. But then, after setting our houses in order, we can relax and enjoy our remaining years.

Jesus was facing his own death and he knew that his disciples would endure uncertainties and even martyrdom in the future. And yet he spoke to them about God's abiding love: "I have said these things to you so that my joy may be in you, and that your joy may be complete" (John 15:11).

34 "We Promised!"

When my Dad reached the age of ninety-two, he realized that he could no longer live alone four miles out in the country. He gave me "durable power of attorney" but was determined to make his own living arrangements. When I suggested that he could live with Jim and me, he was firm: "No, your mother and I promised each other that we would never move in with one of our children. We know how hard it was when Grandma came to live with us."

Many adult children face a problem when two or three generations try to live together. Sometimes it is the best solution; more often it is not. I tried to help Dad find other solutions, such as getting someone to live with him. Again, he was firm. "No," he said, "I don't want any stranger moving in here."

A neighbor woman would have come in for four hours each weekday, but when he found out what it would cost, he said, "I might as well go into the nursing home. I know a lot of people there and I can use the nursing home insurance that I've paid into for years."

Unfortunately, the night before he entered I read for the first time the fine print of that policy. True, it was with a reputable company, but he could not meet the necessary three-day-hospital stay and Medicare-certified room requirements. (Better long-term care policies are now available, and I have signed up for one.)

So long as Dad was ambulatory, able to live on the "good wing," he was fairly happy. To test his decision, we invited him one Thanksgiving to ride the 500 miles in our comfortable van to our home in Oklahoma. Again he said, "No, we promised. . . ."

I assured him that it was not to live permanently but just to visit until Christmas. During those four weeks, I have never seen anyone more homesick. He had lived all his life on a farm just eight miles from the nursing home. It was like trying to transplant a weak and withering plant to new soil. And so we returned him to his new home, having learned that sheltered living in an institution may be the best solution for some. I resigned myself to being a long-distance caregiver, driving the 500 miles to visit every month or two.

Dr. Elizabeth Kübler-Ross states that the two main anxieties of terminal patients are the fear of being a burden to others and concern about how loved ones will care for themselves after the patient's death.[1]

Although Dad was probably too independent for his own good, I realize that his concern was for me, as well as for himself. What a great gift he gave to me when he said, "We promised!" His love gave me freedom to pursue my own life's dreams.

I have already placed my name on the eligible list at a Christian retirement center. When my daughter went with me to see a one-bedroom apartment, she frowned. “Mother, it’s awfully small!”

"Yes,” I said, “but it’s a lot bigger than your Grandpa’s room with a roommate in the nursing home.” I should have added that I have promised myself never to become a burden to her.

35 *Senior Obedience School*

A friend says, "My daughter tells me that I should buy some new clothes. Why? I have enough to last another twenty years. When did we become our children's children?"

When my girls were entering grade school, I would daily point to at least two different outfits. "Which do you want to wear today?" They thought they had choices—but they were limited. It kept them from wearing bare midriffs or skirts too short.

Now as I become older, I realize that they may some day have to limit my choices. They might have to tell me to buy new clothes, although they know I would enjoy that! More likely, it would be to take away my car keys or otherwise curtail my freedoms.

I hope that when I become more dependent on my children that they will continue to give me the right to choose in as many ways as possible. On the other hand, I must prepare them for the fact that if I become one of the "frail" old I will need them. They know how independent I am and that I might become even more set in my ways. I pray that God will give me the grace to accept what I cannot change and to tolerate restrictions I do not like.

Have you seen Charlie Brown's dog at his typewriter in the *Peanuts* comic strip? "I'm an old dog now," he wrote, "I'm not a puppy anymore. But my life isn't over. There are places to go, things to do, and lots still to learn."

But then the dog spoiled it all by adding the line: "So he enrolled in Senior Obedience School."

Our going and doing may become restricted, but so long as we are rational we should be allowed to take some risks. We can continue to travel while packing a heating pad and a container of pills. Airlines even have good wheelchair assistance.

I remember the enjoyable cruise to Alaska that Jim and I took just one year before his death. He had suffered a light stroke about four weeks before our departure date. Our trip could not be canceled, and some older women in our church were depending on us to accompany them. His doctor was uncertain whether he should go because of residual weakness in his right leg. But the physical therapist advised us: "Go! There are doctors and hospitals everywhere. I believe in being a risk taker." It proved to be a wonderful relaxing cruise, and Jim was glad for an excuse to stay aboard rather than visit the ports-of-call with their souvenir shops.

And so, I believe in being as independent as possible. I don't know where we draw the line, but I like the poem which begins, "When I am an old lady I shall wear purple, with a red hat which doesn't go . . . I shall sit down on the pavement when I am tired . . . And run my stick along the public railings and make up for the sobriety of my youth. . . ."[1]

I am not enrolled in Obedience School yet.

36 "Who Needs Me? I Don't Have Anyone!"

Elizabeth Patty, the youngest of seven children, came at age eleven with her widowed mother and siblings on a sailing boat from the Isle of Man (Irish Sea). At age twenty she was married to Gus Schnake, also the youngest of a large family. Hence she lived all of her adult life surrounded by many older relatives as well as friends.

Elizabeth was my grandmother. After Grandpa died in 1935, a son and daughter-in-law moved into the large two-story farmhouse with her. She seemed to be happy as she helped create an efficiency apartment out of the old parlor, which had been furnished with antiques and opened only for the visit of her minister or other very important people. She willingly gave most of her furniture to her children and helped arrange her new living space, which she would occupy for twelve years, until her death at age ninety-one.

"I don't have anyone anymore!" I was startled when I heard Grandma make that statement. She always seemed to enjoy the frequent visits of her four children, thirteen grandchildren, and a growing number of great grandchildren. She did not seem to be depressed. She never lost her little chuckle. I did not understand.

Not have anyone anymore? I felt like saying, "Well, what about us? Don't we count?"

Family does count. Friends count. But Grandma was the only one left of her generation. Lifelong friends had died. There was no one with whom she could share memories of early years.

She had also lost that feeling of being needed. She could no longer host family reunions or even take care of daily household chores. She had become a dependent, with little purpose for living—except to visit Richview cemetery. I remember helping her cut flowers from her garden on the day before each Decoration Day. We tied them into bouquets and walked hundreds of feet to place them on dozens of graves.

I regret that I did not ask her to tell me stories about those loved ones—about how her father had died following an explosion in a lead mine, how she had crossed the Atlantic in a sailing boat, how the family had come to Illinois, what her children who had died were like, and how her faith had helped her. She had so much wisdom to share, and I did not ask her for it. Then she would have felt needed.

John Tebbel in *The Courage to Grow Old* describes how Grandma must have felt: "Growing old is like living on an island which gradually grows smaller and smaller. I am aware of the shrinkage—the contraction of foreseeable time in which I may, if lucky, continue to inhabit my island."[1]

He went on to say that if he could take but one book to the desert island it would be the Bible.

Grandma's was well worn. She went with her family every Sunday morning to our little country church, kneeling in prayer beside her pew. It must have been her faith—the Christ of that book—that kept her going.

37 Make Me an Instrument of Your Healing

Doctor Albert Schweitzer, "the saint of the jungle" in Africa, is still lifted up as a supreme instrument for God's healing. With doctorates in philosophy, music and theology, as well as medicine, he ministered to thousands. However, when foreign correspondent Barrett McGurn visited Schweitzer at age eighty-eight in Lambaréné, McGurn reported that the doctor was not making much progress on a new manuscript, that senility and writer's block was overcoming this great man.[1]

Physical powers do decline, faster in some than in others. Until we become aware of our own declining abilities, it's easy to give the wrong slant on aging.

One respected writer, William E. Hulme, observes that most literature on the older years is written in too positive a vein because the authors are in their late fifties and early sixties. They lack genuine knowledge and try to be optimistic about what's ahead.[2]

When I was sixty-five, I thought I was an authority on aging. Hadn't I attended a lot of conferences on the subject? And wasn't I working with older people? Now, ten years later, I question my wisdom. Now I know that I am not an authority but that I am one of the "old" (I hope to become still older). I did not wake up suddenly to this realization. The last stages of life develop gradually from the previous ones. Death, I think, will be simply another passage on a very meaningful journey.

Of course there are physical losses. I have bifocals, I'm about to get hearing aids, and I can't walk as briskly as I would like. As I slow down, I have developed more dependence on God and an inner peace that losses cannot take away. I think that I have a stronger desire to help others along the way.

It may be that most of us wrestle with aging somewhat in the way that Jacob wrestled with a man until daybreak (Genesis 32:24), but then received God's blessing. Indeed, we can go back a few steps with Jacob to Bethel where he dreamed that there was a ladder "set upon the earth, the top of it reaching to heaven... "Surely," Jacob said, "the LORD was in this place—and I did not know it" (Genesis 28:12, 16). Sometimes God is with us on our journey and we may not be aware of his presence.

Believing that God wants us to be instruments of his peace, we can pray with Saint Francis of Assisi:

O Divine Master,
grant that I may not so much seek
to be consoled as to console;
to be understood, as to understand;
to be loved, as to love;
for it is in giving that we receive,
it is in pardoning that we are pardoned,
and it is in dying that we are born to eternal life.

38 God's Waiting Room

Picture the waiting room of a busy doctor. One child running all over the place. Another whining on her mother's lap. Still another with face hidden, crying in fear of the coming needle. Then there are the parents comparing notes, each with a different tale of woe.

Sometimes we may look like that in God's waiting room, not waiting patiently for his healing strength, but rather complaining to all who will listen. We even pout and whine to our own families.

I am not without guilt. I was disappointed this past Christmas when my children all decided to spend Christmas Eve in their own homes. It had been so much fun the year before with grandchildren in sleeping bags all over my family room floor. I already had prepared Christmas stockings for this year. Feeling sorry for myself, I was about ready to call the whole gang up and voice my frustration, when my eyes fell upon a scrap of paper headed "Tips for the Widowed":

- Don't insist on family gatherings all the time
- Don't try to buy consideration
- Don't offer advice
- Concentrate on one-on-one
- Add new interests to your own life.

Then I remembered. Didn't I once even advise my kids that they must develop their own family traditions?

I looked again at the plaque on my bathroom wall: "There are but two lasting bequests we can give our children. The first is roots—the last, wings." So . . . I flew off to one of their homes for a happy Christmas celebration.

John Wesley had no children, but he understood old age. He wrote in his journal on June 28, 1789:

> This day I enter my eighty-sixth year. I now find I grow old. . . . What I should be afraid of is, if I took thought for the morrow, that my body should weigh down my mind; and create either stubbornness, by the decrease of understanding; or peevishness, by the increase of bodily infirmities; but Thou shalt answer for me, O Lord my God.

God has answered for you and me through the words of the psalmist: "I waited patiently for the LORD; he inclined to me and heard my cry. He drew me up from the desolate pit, out of the miry bog, and set my feet upon a rock, making my steps secure. He put a new song in my mouth, a song of praise to our God (Psalm 40:1-3).

Maybe the "desolate pit" and the "miry bog" mean giving way to pettiness, hurts, and disappointments. But God forgives us and, like a mother who comforts her child, puts a new song in our mouth. God's waiting room is a place of peace and praise.

39 Time to Reach Out

The little boy was chatting with his grandfather: "I don't ever want to get old," he declared, " 'cause I won't be able to do lots of stuff anymore."

"Grampa" knew just what to reply, "Let me tell you, son. Some folks do their best work when they get old. Why at eighty-nine, Albert Schweitzer headed a hospital in Africa. George Burns won an academy award at the age of eighty. At 100, Grandma Moses was a famous painter."

The boy looked at him, puzzled, "How about you, Grampa?"

"Me?" The old man thought for a moment, "I set the clock on the VCR all by myself the other day."[1]

I am embarrassed. I don't even know how to set the clock on my oven . . . or how to set the chimes on my grandfather's old Seth Thomas mantle clock. But I haven't called it quits. I taught myself to type at age fifty (although I still don't know the number reaches). At seventy-five, I began to learn to use the word processor. Now I have graduated to the internet and e-mail.

I guess I need to find new ways I can reach out to others. I can't turn back the clock and do what I used to do, or at the same speed. However, I can wind the clock up again, at least reset and plug it in! I can bring some cheer to the sick or grieving, take food to the homebound, be a grandparent to a forlorn child, lend a listening ear to a trouble youth or young parent. God gives me the channels for helping when I lift up to God the needs of those about me, not to mention those in faraway places. Through my computer, maybe I can even do my best work as I get older!

When Chicago's Cardinal Joseph Bernardin was dying of liver cancer in the autumn of 1996, he continued to reach out to others. He determined to use whatever time was left "in a way that will be of benefit to the priests and people I have been called to serve." He gave away money, objects of art and other things he thought were more materialistic than spiritual. Although he came to see death as a friend, he never gave up in his service for others. When he went to the hospital for chemotherapy, he stayed to visit and encourage other patients of all religious backgrounds, or none. He liked to say, "I am Joseph, your brother."[2]

William Hulme, a Presbyterian minister, was correct in observing that vintage years bring a deeper insight into spiritual realities: Greater trust, greater patience, inner peace, inner dialogue with God, an appreciation of the eternal dimension to life—plus values to give our grandchildren. "Grandparents seem to enjoy their grandchildren," he said, "more than parents enjoy their children. . . . We give them unconditional love."[3]

We know many people who need that kind of unconditional love. No matter our age, it is time to reach out.

40 Angels "Whirling Above My Head"

In December of 1994, nine months before the loss of Lance Webb, angels must have been watching over him lest he "dash his foot against a stone." Doctors had been unable to find a cause for the increasing congestion below his heart. Their only solution was Prednisone, which made his walking unsteady, but his faith remained strong.

He often told me how when his first wife Elizabeth was about to undergo emergency surgery—from which she did not recover—she clasped his hand to say, "I'll see you in the morning or I will be with the angels." Thus it was that he came to believe that angels were real, not just symbolic. Because I had known Elizabeth as a friend, even as Lance had known my Jim, we were able to understand and share our experiences.

That autumn had been a difficult time for us both as Lance tried so very hard to regain his strength. One Sunday evening in early December, we listened to his favorite Christmas music. We went to bed with the triumphant sounds of "Angels We Have Heard on High" ringing in our ears.

Even though "Gloria in excelsis Deo!" remained in my unconscious mind, I had trouble falling asleep. I got up to read. Maybe it was my guardian angel who led me to the December *Guideposts* and to the article entitled "A Whirling Above My Head."

In a beautiful letter to Mrs. Norman Vincent Peale, the writer described how on Christmas Eve she had a vision of thousands of angels singing alleluias in glorious voices. She felt the way a child does, she said, when something impossibly wonderful has happened. This puzzling vision lasted most of the night, but not until after she arose did she learn that Dr. Peale had died that night and that she must have witnessed part of the heavenly celebration.[1]

Norman Vincent Peale was a minister who had reached out to many; he was ninety-five years of age, pastor of Marble Collegiate Church for fifty of those years, and first editor of *Guideposts*. He had traveled thousands of miles even after the age of ninety. At his memorial service, his widow Ruth Stafford Peale affirmed; "I believe Norman is having a great time with the angels up there."

Peace came to my heart after I listened again to "Angels We Have Heard on High." I wrote these words in my journal: "I believe that, when the time has fully come, Lance, too, will be escorted to heaven by the angels. Like his friend Norman Vincent Peale, and also like Elizabeth and Jim, he will be 'having a great time with the angels up there.' "

> This is our promise: "He will command
> his angels concerning you to guard you in all your ways.
> On their hands they will bear you up,
> so that you will not dash your foot against a stone."
>
> (Psalm 91:11, 12)

41 *He Guides Us... and the Birds*

How does God guide us? William Cullen Bryant found his answer years ago as he watched a migrating waterfowl:

He who, from zone to zone,
Guides through the boundless sky thy certain flight,
In the long way that I must tread alone
Will lead my steps aright.

For many, it's the reassurance that comes when we watch the geese fly south. Always flying in perfect formation, an unseen hand gives them direction and guidance.

For Lance and me in the last months of his life, the hummingbirds were the tiny creatures who gave us joy and hope. Through the windowed walls of our house high above Beaver Lake, we watched as a few birds increased in number from two to two dozen, greedily drinking nectar from the feeders hanging above the deck. They put on a daily aerial ballet, as if they knew that Lance, too, would soon fly away.

His doctor had already told him to put his affairs in order. For him, that meant completing one manuscript and revising another. During his long ministry, he had written twelve books, but his creative mind was still at work, even though slowing down.

He was now too weak to sit at his computer, but he would not give up. And so, after time in intensive care and near death twice in the hospital, he came home to be supervised by fine hospice nurses, who visited twice a week.

He sat at the table—watching the birds—five times a day, and continued to stumble around the deck in an effort to regain his strength. He was losing weight, like a small plane throwing off gasoline to gain ascension. "I've got to call my doctor," he insisted, "to find out why I'm not getting stronger."

When the good doctor called he was honest, explaining, "Your heart, the body's engine, is just worn out. It's like trying to drive to Kansas City with a frayed fan belt. You might make it and you might not. No one else would have made it this far."

For the first time, Lance accepted the truth, although he still mentioned manuscripts before he hung up. He did begin to talk more about his parents and deceased sister and brothers, as well as Elizabeth and Jim. "I guess I've got more loved ones on the other side than here, and I'm ready for a joyous reunion—but I've got to complete those manuscripts!"

After I struggled one night to lift him off the floor and back into our bed, he asked: "You're not going to ditch me, are you?" I quickly reassured him, "Of course not, I'm with you all the way to the Pearly Gates, only they probably won't let me in."

He knew that he had disobeyed orders when he had groped his way into our dressing room to get a warm robe instead of waking me. I put my arms around his frail body, and he fell into a fitful sleep, murmuring, "Let's go home." I think he meant our heavenly home.

His wish was granted early Saturday, September 9. I was glad to greet Joan, an excellent nurse, who had been monitoring his heart. I met her outside to report that Lance had been semicomatose all night, not speaking, but not suffering—lying still on the hospital bed in the living room. I had slept nearby on the sofa, waking every hour to make sure he was still breathing. Each time, I patted his face, trying to get him to speak to me. I asked him to squeeze my hand if he could hear me, but there was no response.

Joan observed immediately that his skin color was changing and that the end was near. She also noted how stiffly his hands were folded across his chest. She bent over his body, "Oh, Bishop Webb, you have been such a blessing to the world. We'll never forget you. When I get home, I'm going to finish reading your book. You will live on through your books. It's all right.... It's all right, Bishop Webb, to let go." His hands relaxed! A few more breaths and he did let go, with a smile on his face.

When I returned home alone after a beautiful memorial service in Dallas, I dreaded entering the empty house. But when I stepped over to the place where the hospital bed had been, I sensed a peace that passes understanding.

I looked through the glass doors to see the hummingbirds. They were all gone, on their way flying 500 miles south! Maybe they had taken a detour to give Lance a winged escort to heaven—symbolically, yes! Love surrounded him on the flight of his soul to God!

42 "I Carried You"

Sometimes the way gets to be too much for us and we become discouraged, as was the man in the widely read poem. He had a dream one night, a dream that flashed scenes of his own life before his eyes, and he was puzzled. He could see two sets of footprints when his Lord had walked with him on the pathway of life. But then he noticed the many times when there was only one set of footprints—the lowest and saddest times of his life. He asked why. "Lord," he said, "I don't understand why when I needed you most you would leave me."

"My precious child," the Lord replied, "I love you and would never leave you. During your times of trial and suffering, when you see only one set of footprints, it was then that I carried you" (from "Footprints," author unknown).

God understands our human frailties and knows when we need some extra attention; there is only so much that our bodies can take. That was the experience of Elijah in the Old Testament story, when the exhausted prophet was fleeing from the wicked Queen Jezebel. Elijah had not only fled for his life, but had gone by himself an extra day's journey into the wilderness, ready to give up.

Elijah asked God to let him die as he fell asleep under a tree. Twice an angel awakened him, bringing him food to eat and water to drink. The command was "Get up and eat, otherwise the journey will be too much for you."

God knows when the journey has become too much for us. God carries us where we need to go, just as he gave Elijah the strength to "go out and stand on the mountain" to hear his voice, even in the "sound of sheer silence" (1 Kings 19:4-12).

Our Heavenly Father does not desert us when we need him most. Even in death, many have been able to say along with John Wesley, "The best of all: God is with us!" Assurance comes at the end of the journey. We begin to think more about loved ones who have gone on ahead of us. We can liken it to a "cloud of witnesses" in the grandstand cheering us onward.

The Letter to the Hebrews names many who have died in the faith: "Therefore, since we are surrounded by so great a cloud of witnesses, let us lay aside every weight and the sin that clings so closely, and let us run with perseverance the race that is set before us, looking unto Jesus the pioneer and perfector of our faith, who for the sake of the joy that was set before him endured the cross, disregarding its shame, and has taken his seat at the right hand of the throne of God" (Hebrews 12:1-2).

> Come, let us join our friends above who have obtained the prize
> and on the eagle wings of love to joys celestial rise.
> Let saints on earth unite to sing with those in glory gone,
> for all the servants of our King in earth and heaven are one.
>
> (Charles Wesley)

43 *The Journey to Jesus*

An often overlooked part of the Christmas story is that of the old man Simeon, who had waited long in the Temple to see the Messiah. When the child Jesus was brought in "he took him in his arms and blessed God" (Luke 2:28) in words that have become the *Nunc Dimittis* of the church universal:

> Lord, now let your servant go in peace;
> your word has been fulfilled:
> my own eyes have seen the salvation
> which you have prepared in the presence of all people,
> a light to reveal you to the nations
> and the glory of your people Israel.

Simeon had a powerful dream. So did the Wise Men. So did Mary and Joseph. And so do we!

The star still shines over Bethlehem as it did two thousand years ago. Better yet, that star shines in our hearts today. We pray that we may seek and find, as the Wise Men did, the Christ of eternity.

Christmas and heaven meet within our hearts, and the dream becomes clearer in the light of Christ's love. He was "born that we no more may die, born to raise us from the earth. . . . 'Glory to the newborn King.' "

****

It is Christmas now in the Ozarks. I no longer sit out on the deck, but looking out from my cozy house, through the picture window, I am surprised by a beautiful scene this morning. A soft blanket of new-fallen snow has covered the barren rocks, the sleeping grasses and frozen bushes. It came so silently that I can scarcely believe it.

Only yesterday, a few dead leaves were still clinging to the overhanging branches of my huge oak tree; now they are covered with what looks like puffy cotton balls. The cedars are bowed down with the weight, as if in humble prayer. Other trees glisten as the rising sun makes a thin coat of ice begin to sparkle. It is a jeweled wonderland.

This is the time of wonder, the season of the star! We sing about the beauty of the earth, even as we remember that we are here to observe the coming of our Savior:

> For thyself, best Gift Divine, to the world so freely given,
> for that great, great love of thine, peace on earth, and joy in heaven:
> Lord of all, to thee we raise this our hymn of grateful praise.
>
> (Folliot S. Pierpoint)

We have watched his star rise in the heavens. God hung it there for the ages. Its radiance has guided us on our earthly journey, and it will guide us at last to Jesus. God, give us eyes this Christmas to see the Christmas star!

Notes, Thoughts, Prayers

Notes, Thoughts, Prayers

Notes, Thoughts, Prayers

Notes, Thoughts, Prayers

End Notes

2. Gathering the Autum Fruit

1. Elton Trueblood, as quoted in *The Courage to Grow Old,* Phillip L. Berman, ed. (New York: Ballantine Books, 1989), pp. 293-94.

3. Miles to Go Before I Sleep

1. Harold Bell Wright, *Shepherd of the Hills* (The Shepherd of the Hills Historical Society, Inc., 1907), p, 1.
2. Dante: *Inferno I,* 1-3.
3. Robert Frost: "Stopping By Woods."

5. Becoming Older Rather Than Old

1. Art Linkletter, *Old Age Is Not for Sissies* (New York: Viking Penguin, 1988), p. 22.
2. Richard H. Gentzler Jr. and Donald F. Clingan, *Aging: God's Challenge to Church and Synagogue* (Nashville: Discipleship Resources), p. 8.
3. Alfred Lord Tennyson: *Ulysses.*

8. Going Down the Valley One-by-One

1. Gentzler and Clingan, *Aging,* p. 18.

9. A New Landscape with Grief

1. As quoted in *On Being Alone,* the AARP Guide for Widowed Persons.

14. If Only! If Only!

1. Gail Sheehy, *New Passages* (New York: Random House, 1995), p. 142.

21. To Love Again?

1. Lance Webb, as quoted in "Two Roads Converge," unpublished manuscript by Marie White Webb.

22. Don't Make Me Laugh!

1. Linkletter, *Old Age Is Not for Sissies,* p. 16.
2. Sheehy, *New Passages,* p. 11.

27. Fight the Good Fight

1. William Barclay, *The Letters to Timothy, Titus and Philemon* (Philadelphia: Westminster Press, 1956), p. 243.

28. Tomorrow Is a Dream That Leads Me Onward

1. Robert Browning: "Rabbi Ben Ezra," stanza 1.
2. Dylan Thomas credit to come
3. Berman, *The Courage to Grow Old,* xii.

29. Enroute on the Christmas Journey

1. Elisabeth Kübler-Ross, *Death: The Final Stage of Growth* (Englewood Cliffs, NJ: Prentice Hall, 1975), p. 73.

34. "We Promised!"

1. Kübler-Ross, *Death: The Final Stages of Growth,* p. 80.

35. Senior Obedience School

1. Jenny Joseph, "Warning," a poem quoted in *When I Am an Old Woman,* Sandra Mertz, ed. (Watsonville, Calif.: Papiér-Mache Press, 1987), p. 1.

36. "Who Needs Me? I Don't Have Anyone!"

1. Berman, *The Courage to Grow Old,* p. 161.

37. Make Me an Instrument of Your Healing

1. *Berman, The Courage to Grow Old,* p. 118.
2. William E. Hulme, *Vintage Years* (Philadelphia: Westminster Press, 1986), p. 36.

39. Time to Reach Out

1. As quoted in "Pickles," Brian Cane Cartoon strip (Washington Post Writers Group, 1/19/97).
2. Kenneth L. Woodward and John McCormick, "The Art of Dying Well," *Newsweek,* November 25, 1996, pp. 61-66.
3. Hulme, *Vintage Years,* 74-78.

40. Angels "Whirling Above My Head"

1. Marjorie Martin, "A Whirling Above My Head," *Guideposts,* December 1994, p. 53.